THE
NEWS
IS

Evangelism as a Way of Life

JEFF STARK

GOOD

f·

THE FOUNDRY
PUBLISHING°

Cover design: J.R. Caines
Interior design: Sharon Page

Library of Congress Cataloging-in-Publication Data

A complete catalog record for this book is available from the Library of Congress.

The internet addresses, email addresses, and phone numbers in this
book are accurate at the time of publication. They are provided as a re-
source. The Foundry Publishing does not endorse them or vouch for their
content or permanence.

10 9 8 7 6 5 4 3 2 1

CONTENTS

INTRODUCTION

Therefore go and make disciples of all nations, baptizing them in the name of the Father and of the Son and of the Holy Spirit, and teaching them to obey everything I have commanded you. And surely I am with you always, to the very end of the age.

—Matthew 28:19–20

The church does not just send out missionaries to faraway lands; the church, as it is situated in a specific context, is sent by God to be good news in its surroundings.[1]

●————————————————●

Before you begin this journey, there are two disclaimers I must make on the front end. Without these two disclaimers, something might get lost along the way.

First, I absolutely, wholeheartedly, without a shadow of a doubt believe that the story of Jesus is *good news*. In fact, I would say it is the best news ever shared throughout the whole of

---

1. Al Tizon, *Missional Preaching: Engage, Embrace, Transform* (Valley Forge, PA: Judson Press, 2012), xxii.

human history. Jesus Christ is the hinge on which all of human history swings. I'm utterly captivated and compelled by the whole gospel of Jesus, and I seek to live my life—in woefully inadequate and imperfect ways—in alignment with and as an expression of this good news. I also believe it's news that can't be kept to myself. It's news that beckons us to share it where we can, when we can, and with whom we have the opportunity. As a follower of Jesus, I'm an evangelist—not as a unique calling, a particular task, or a specific function of the church but instead as one who is called to live genuinely, authentically, and faithfully as what I like to call a "good newser." That's all evangelism is for me—living genuinely in accordance with the story of faith that has transformed my life in a way that leads others to ask, "So what's your deal? Why are you like that?" Notably, when I betray the good news by living out of alignment with the story or adopting other stories that aren't such good news (see chapter 3), I feel deeply remorseful because life as a good newser is both a privilege and a responsibility.

Second, this book is *not* a how-to guide. If that's what you were looking for, sorry. There are no surefire ways or approaches to "win friends and influence others." There are no tactics to turn a conversation into a conversion. I can't guarantee that reading this book will make you able to close the deal with that person you've been meeting with a few times a month. Books and trainings on evangelism that begin with the assumption that we must learn how to close the deal already begin at the point of disingenuousness. Evangelism is *not* a sales pitch! Evangelism is authenticity in action. It's living before others, valuing others, extending dignity to others, being curious about others—in a way that connects the core of the Christian hope with the presence of Christian love in beautifully redemptive ways. When you do so, you will find you won't need a pitch. You won't need to manipulate a conversation. Evangelism will become a natural, organic expression of living true to the gospel story. This is about *lifestyle*, not about *methodology*.

A Defining Moment

Later, I will share a bit more of my story of stepping into this new life of following Jesus. However, on the front end let me say that I came to faith at the age of twenty-five in a small army chapel in Skopje, Macedonia, in 2001—and was then taught to walk in the ways of Jesus by some of the most amazing men of faith. The U.S. Army calls them chaplains, but I call them gifts from God. It was like lighting a fire in dry brush. I was on fire for Jesus from the very beginning. This Jesus had singlehandedly stepped in and rescued me from the depths of my dysfunction and offered me new life. I was hooked, and I wanted everyone to know it.

Not long after that, I was having clumsy conversations with colleagues and coworkers about Jesus. Shortly afterward, I was in my first personal evangelism training class, taught by a woman who was passionate to see people come to faith. I'll discuss a little more about the lineage of my evangelistic fervor momentarily. I was having conversations with people in my home; at G's Pancake House across from Gate 1 at Fort Campbell, Kentucky; in the motor pool; and wherever else someone would grant me the time of day. These conversations all had varying levels of success. The frequency of conversation often depends on the context of one's situation. God conversations (especially Jesus conversations) seem to be more common, more expected, in the Bible Belt of Tennessee than they are perhaps in the coffee shops of Portland, the corporate hubs of Palo Alto, or the boroughs of New York City.

In my fervor, I had also stepped into leading our college ministry outreach at the church I attended. Having absolutely no idea what I was doing, and with about six students from Austin Peay State University in tow, we headed to The Potter's House in Springfield, Missouri. Home to Missouri State University, Springfield was also home to Steve and Berna. They, like many good newsers I've met, weren't celebrities, yet they have lived lives of faith with an influence that extends to the far reaches of the globe because they opened a coffee house across the street from the university campus and set up shop. There, they lived and worked as faithful good newsers.

On one of the nights of our visit, Steve pulled me outside and asked if he could introduce me to someone. I followed him to a table where a chessboard was set up, and he introduced me to a young man named Kabir who had a thick beard and wore a turban. Kabir was a Sikh from India whom Steve had befriended through The Potter's House and could be found on nearly any Friday night educating Steve on chess (which is a polite way of saying, beating Steve—badly). Steve told me they had a running challenge: if Steve were to beat Kabir in a game of chess, Kabir would allow Steve to share the gospel with him.

As I observed their friendly game, Steve asked Kabir to share with me his experience of Christians since arriving in the United

States. Kabir said, "Jeff, since I've been in the States and land-ed at this campus, nearly every campus ministry has at some point come up to me and tried to get me saved. They all have their pitches and talking points. But I've come to believe that if this news is as good as you say it is, well, you wouldn't have to try to sell it to people—you should just be able to *give* it away." Boom—mic drop (before mic drops were even cool).

As he said this, two things happened. First, Steve and I looked at each other with a profound sense of *"that* just happened." Second, I played in my mind the number of times I'd used a canned approach in the name of Jesus. I had applied learned tactics that I was convinced were genuine concern for the souls of the people with whom I shared, but in retrospect, these speeches and tactics may have felt to the listeners no different than a pitch for a pyramid scheme. Had the people I'd ap-proached felt loved, heard, or valued? Had I taken time to get to know them, see them, ensure that they knew they mattered to me? Had I based our relationship on a religious transaction? *Was I a Jesus salesman?*

A Little Grace for Methodological Imperfection

The answers to all of these questions were: *sometimes, maybe, yes,* and *maybe more than I would like to admit.* In short, I had done the best I could with what I had and as much as I knew at the time. Still today, there *are* people following Jesus from that season of my life. This is why I'm not a throw-the-baby-out-with-the-bathwater kind of guy. God works despite our imperfection and in partnership with our genuine intentions. Someone's salvation is always occasioned by God's grace to the recipient of the good news and not the approach. God has used, and still uses, street-corner preachers and little tracts of paper that look like dollar bills (every time I meet someone who became a Jesus follower this way, I'm still astounded—only God!). God has used stadium conferences, bridge diagrams, wordless books, artistic illustrations, and formulaic representations—all of which I've been trained on and have at some point used.

The soul-searching Kabir's comment set off in me didn't lead me to conclude that all evangelism is bad. Instead, it forced me to ask myself, "How can I ensure that the good news of Jesus—a news that has radically changed my life—flows from such a genuine, authentic, vulnerable, relational place that the person listening is blessed and encouraged?"

A Good-Newsing Lineage

One of the reasons I was able to hold onto this tension of being deeply committed to the work of evangelism and a dissatisfaction with my practice and current methods is due to the community of faith to which I belonged. My first church as a Jesus follower—the church where I would begin my vocational ministry—was filled with genuine good newsers. Evangelism wasn't then and isn't now a theoretical problem to be solved—it was a regular practice of godly men and women who mentored me in faith and left their holy imprint on numerous lives. Clarksville First Church of the Nazarene was ground zero for me about why evangelism mattered. Daily I bumped up against the lives of men and women who had been transformed by the redeeming grace of Jesus, baptized members of God's people, and missional agents deployed into the world to shine a bit of light.

The evidence of evangelistic fervor was undeniable. I'd filled too many baptisteries over a nine-year period (and flooded one gymnasium—but that's a different story!) to be able to deny the impact of genuine good newsing.

It was evident in my pastor's life. In September 2001, while I remained deployed, my wife knelt in Pastor Kim's office and received the grace of forgiveness and became a Jesus follower. He signed and gave her a heart's door card, and it remained on our mirror in the bathroom for nearly fifteen years afterward.[2] Evangelism made Kim come alive. He had this uncanny capacity to sit in a living room with someone who'd started checking out our church, ask a few questions about their lives, and by the second cup of coffee they'd be asking, "What must we do to be saved?" For Kim, it wasn't canned. It was genuine. He wept with them. He hugged them. He baptized them. He knew their names. He walked alongside them. There were few things that brought Kim more joy than watching as God welcomed home one of his own.

I witnessed it in the life of twice-retired man's man, Ron. Ron had retired from the army and from being a cop, so as you can imagine, Ron was a real touchy-feely kind of guy—hardly! Did I mention that Ron also rode a Harley? Ron and I started on staff about the same time at Clarksville First, but before that he'd been one of my mentors. He gave me my first church job:

---

2. The phrase "heart's door card" refers to the pocket-size cards that depict Warner Sallman's famous painting *Christ at Heart's Door*. Such cards can be viewed and purchased in bulk from The Foundry Publishing, https://www.thefoundrypublishing.com/jesus-knocking-hearts-door-pocket-card-aw-250.html.

egg stirrer at the men's prayer breakfast. Ron had that kitchen operating like a tight military outfit, allowing me to move up to sausage flipper only after I demonstrated months of faithful egg stirring. Ron's sometimes bristly personality made him perfect for a unique ministry to bikers. I too had been in the army, but I also sang in musicals, wore plaid sweater vests, and once frosted the tips of my hair—bikers would have eaten me for lunch! But not Ron. Ron embedded himself in a group of people, many of whom had limited access to Jesus. He rode with them, loved them, hung out with them, went to where they were. He dressed like them, cared for them, learned about them, and shared Jesus with them. He would eventually plant a church in his late sixties called Hope Riders.

I was discipled (trained to follow Jesus) by a forty-five-year-old, electric-pole-climbing, gigantic man whose forearms were the size of my head. Bearing a striking resemblance to a bearded Mr. Clean, Earl took my wife, Angie, and me under his wing, helping us on the front end of our journey make sense of what all this Jesus-following stuff was about. Earl had a clear sense of purpose. Regularly on Thursday nights when he'd come to our house to disciple us, he'd tell us, "I know my purpose. Luke 19:10: 'to seek and to save the lost.' And to glorify God in all I do." When you are discipled by someone who states that their life mission is Luke 19:10, it can't help but affect you.

I wanted to be like Earl when I grew up—with perhaps more hair. Earl's passion for people worked through everything he did. He wept for those who felt disconnected from Jesus at the altar. He was the first to help newcomers feel like they had arrived home. He longed for the moment when God afforded him the opportunity to tell someone—anyone—about all that God had done for him and what God could do for them. There is no telling the number of people who have been good newsed into the kingdom of God through Earl. Earl had a hand in discipling more than a dozen pastors whose ministries now span the globe.

I witnessed it in the life of my friend Brett, who was hired in 2006 to serve as our pastor of compassionate ministry. Brett's evangelistic fervor was different from the soul-winning energy of Pastor Ruth, who had trained me in evangelistic tools. Both cared about people coming to faith, but those to whom Brett felt called required an approach that stretched the limitations of my prior training. Brett recognized that one couldn't speak to the salvation of the soul and remain unconcerned about the conditions of their lives. Brett's good newsing required a deeply incarnational approach, where the holy presence of Jesus was evidenced through the patient, faithful, tender, compassionate lives of his followers. Through Brett, my vision of the good news expanded to include concern for the issues and systems that keep people stuck in environments where they are unable to flourish in the ways God intended. Being a good newser meant being an advocate for justice, a feeder of the hungry, a clother of the naked, and someone who set captives free from addiction and compulsion. Being an evangelist meant weekly hangouts with the homeless at the day shelter, launching a nonprofit ministry center to keep people from eviction, and hosting a citywide Christmas celebration for those in need. Those who came to faith through our compassionate ministry did so because of a patient, credible, just witness that was concerned with the whole person.

I could go on and on. I could mention Cliff and Annette, Randy and Vicky, the English saxophonist Tony, Tereva, Marvin and Netra, or Jorge. These men and women regularly displayed a commitment to the good news. This was the peculiar community to which I belonged, made up of people who, for the first nearly nine years of my faith journey, nurtured my belief in the profound power of being a good newser. My reflections on the practice of evangelism were born in a community of faith that bore the evidence of the practice.

Tell Me . . . *That*

One evening as we sat around a charcuterie board, hungry amid the COVID-19 crisis for human connection that reflected the safety measures and mitigation tactics of the time, my Australian friend said, "Tell me . . . *that*." As a couple, they were two of the first people Angie and I met when we settled in our new home in the heart of Chicago. For almost two decades we'd been in pastoral ministry, moved through three different churches, and now found ourselves heeding my call to teach at Olivet Nazarene University and live an hour north in the heart of the city of Chicago as urban missionaries. Having no church awaiting our arrival and a city that could care less that we were there, I asked myself, *Where can I connect with folks?*

I camped out at the local coffee shop (a destination I will return to often throughout this book). There, showing up every day, I connected with Alyssa. This mom of two toddlers was bright, energetic, and full of life. She was kind of known as "the mayor of La Colombe." She knew everyone. I often sat in the same spot with a stack of books. One day she introduced herself, and we hit it off. She and her husband, Ryan, hadn't been in Chicago much longer than Angie and me, so there was a connection there. Besides that, they were one of the coolest families we'd ever met. They'd traveled, lived in multiple countries, and could talk to anyone about nearly anything. As the four of us got to know one another, they ultimately learned I had spent several years as a pastor. To be honest, this isn't the first thing I share about myself in most places, especially in cities where the Bible Belt is missing the leather and the buckle. You generally don't get points for saying, "Yeah, I'm an evangelical pastor!" But friendship brings things out of people.

Both Alyssa and Ryan shared with me that neither of them were particularly keen toward religious faith, though they had nothing explicitly against it. In fact, they ensured their children had religious godparents to facilitate a well-rounded upbringing. They are awesome people and wonderful parents. Though their interest wasn't in religion, we often found ourselves conversing about issues that circled the border areas of religious faith. She occasionally reminded me she was an atheist. Over time, our friendship grew more and more rich. We hung out with them. Their kids brought Angie and me so much joy. I learned from Ryan about global business, and Alyssa's passion for people with disability was inspiring. The four of us just did life together. We dropped off donuts to the kids during COVID lockdowns, and we'd meet for coffee outside on the corner.

One evening, after knowing Ryan and Alyssa for a little over a year, Angie and I were visiting with them around the charcuterie board when they asked us how we met. We can't tell how we met without eventually also talking about how we came to faith. The faith piece has kept us together for more than twenty years. If it hadn't been for Jesus, there wouldn't be an *us* to talk about. So I mentioned that, but in an effort to honor them and not make them feel as if I were cramming religion down their throats, I moved quickly past that part. Alyssa stopped me and said, "Wait! Tell me . . . *that*. I want to hear that piece. How did you go from atheist to religious?"

To be honest, I hadn't seen it coming. But Ryan and Alyssa gave me a gift in that moment. That's the blessing of friendship: reciprocity. That moment wasn't canned, manipulated, or even all that purposeful. It was organic, natural, and the result of life lived together. Ryan and Alyssa valued us enough as friends to let us share something near and dear to our hearts. We spent the next hour sharing our story and talking about the things of God. They were letting me live out my good-newsing self. Two of the best people we knew—people who had invited us into their lives, people we'd met at a coffee shop in a city of 2.7 million people—were now affording us the opportunity to express our faith. What a gift! When you love people enough, they will love you back. They will give you the opportunity to share the things you hold most dear. And that's an immense gift.

Bubbling to the Surface

There's probably one more assumption at work in this book that I need to be honest about on the front end. Evangelism as a lifestyle of good-newsing people only happens if we take seriously the call of Jesus to direct our energy and attention toward those who are disconnected from the hope, healing, and wholeness found in the person of Jesus Christ. And this is a problem. At times along this journey, you might feel as though I'm pestering you, poking around in some uncomfortable spaces, refusing to leave well enough alone. I kinda, sorta apologize for that on the front end (though not really). It's a hazard of my life's work and occupation. I am a missional theologian by trade and training. What does that mean? It means I care deeply about the church's posture, presence, and practices as the church engages the broader world. I make the assumption that, when Jesus challenged us (twice!) with the commission (*co-mission*) of the gospel, he meant what he said! First, in Matthew 25, he seems to suggest that God's people who fail to care about those who are wounded, battered, and left vulnerable by life will be denied the desired favor and blessedness of God's kingdom. Second, in Matthew 28, Jesus seems to suggest that a life spent going into the world should be a life that is deeply committed to cultivating apprentices to Jesus wherever we are. The church is a "so that" community. We are captivated by grace, converted to allegiance to the way of Jesus, and called to join Jesus in what he is up to in this world, *so that* the world might know of his love and redemptive purposes. I can't imagine the church, or my participation in the faith of Christianity, outside of this clear sense of calling.

Unfortunately, in many ways, Christians have abdicated this responsibility, or farmed it out to others. We've unwittingly and unintentionally built a Christian industrial complex that saturates Christians in practices, events, and a subculture that disconnects them from the lives of their neighbors all around them. We've created bubbles (often associated with our buildings) wherein we release people from the pressure of personal engagement and friendship with those outside the Christian faith by offering them a smorgasbord of programming. When this happens, there are two outcomes. First, a non-vocational Christian (one who isn't a pastor or leader in a church) sees their evangelistic responsibility as inviting the unsaved people they know *to church* so that the professionals (the vocational Christians) can do what they are paid to do. (Note: there is so much wrong with the prior sentence that it would take a completely different book to unpack it all!) Second, because we lack organic relationships that are embedded in deeply personal friendships, or because we lack proximity to deeply broken environments, we turn evangelism into another program, a special ministry of the church, or a training with canned approaches. Again, God can use and has used all of this—but I do not believe it is God's preferred mode of operation. God's chosen and preferred mode of operation is you!

I'm advocating for a significant shift—a missional posture for all who call themselves followers of Jesus. The Jesus life is best lived when we recognize that our going out into the world— wherever that going out leads us—is for the purpose of bearing witness to Jesus. Those committed to an apprenticeship to Jesus and to making other apprentices—what Scripture calls disciples—are leery of getting caught up in a bubble. Missional Christians are bubble bursters. We go out into the world, stepping intentionally into the lives of those who are disconnected from faith in Jesus. We go out into the world, stepping intentionally into spaces that have been ravaged by injustice and brokenness. We go out into the world, stepping intentionally into environments that might be otherwise hostile to the things

of God. We go out into the world because following Jesus leads
us there.

And when we go out, making our life's calling our proximity to
and presence with those searching for a hope they can't seem
to articulate, our very living will provide ample opportunities
for our lifestyle of good newsing to bubble up to the surface in
genuine and authentic ways. We will be afforded the chance to
"give an answer to everyone who asks you to give the reason for
the hope that you have. But do this with gentleness and re-
spect, keeping a clear conscience, so that those who speak ma-
liciously against your good behavior in Christ may be ashamed
of their slander" (1 Peter 3:15b–16).

This book emerges against the backdrop of the seasons of my
own life. It is a reflection on my embeddedness in a church that
took seriously the work of evangelism in my formative Jesus
years, my discontent with some of the messaging and methodology of traditional evangelism, and my genuine desire to live in
the city of Chicago as an authentic good newser. Along the way,
I hope to offer to you an opportunity to claim a passion for a
lifestyle of good news.

SECTION 1

Good Starts and Good News

God's mission is to restore the entire creation and the life of humankind to what God intended in the beginning. The goal of God is not to take people out of this world to live as disembodied spirits in heaven but to restore a people to live bodily in the midst of a restored creation. God's mission is not merely to clean up some individuals so they can live with him in heaven but to clean up the creation so he can come back and live here with us. God's mission is to return the world to what it's supposed to be.[1]

●·······················●

For years I played both high school and college American football. For years I coached both middle school and high school American football. All those years taught me many things, but perhaps none as important as this: how we start matters.

I was an offensive lineman and coached offensive linemen. For those uneducated in the ways of American football, offensive

---

1. Michael W. Goheen and Jim Mullins, *The Symphony of Mission: Playing Your Part in God's Work in the World* (Grand Rapids: Baker Academic, 2019), 5.

linemen are those really big, often seemingly out of shape, belly-bursting-out-of-tight-shirt guys who stand in a line shoulder to shoulder and run into the other really large, belly-bursting-out-of-tight-shirt guys directly across from them. We call it the trenches. To the untrained eye, it looks like a chaotic mess of big bodies crashing into one another, attempting to exert strength over their nemeses. The assumption might be that the bigger, stronger, tougher guy always wins the battle in the trenches. But that's not true!

I was a big dude but rarely the biggest. I was a nominally strong dude but never the strongest. However, I rarely got beat. Why? Because, when I started playing football, a coach drilled it into our heads that *how we start matters*. We would, every single practice, spend fifteen to twenty minutes practicing our *first step*. We'd line up. He'd call a play. He'd hike the football. We'd take one step. And then we'd do it again. It had to be precise. The quickness of our first step, the angle of our first step, the distance between our first step and our other foot, the position of our hips, the angle of our arms—all of it mattered. And that was just our first step. My coach was convinced that the battle in the trenches was won in the first step. The lineman with the best first step, the most precise form, the most accurate start, nearly always won the play. How we start matters.

This was no truer than when I was coaching high school football at a small school in rural Tennessee. We barely had enough kids to field a full varsity team at times. Rarely did I have an abundance of gargantuan men waiting to be molded by me into fierce warriors. I made do with what I had. Twice in my years of coaching, two of my best linemen weighed under 160 pounds.

That's almost half the size of some of the adversaries they'd face! Why were they my best linemen? They knew they didn't have the luxury of relying on their size or brute force. How they started mattered. They fine-tuned their first steps on every play. They were the most precise players on the field. They always took the right angle and placed their hips and hands in the right spot. You could say they were the best at what they did because they always began on the right foot.

Evangelism is like American football in that regard. Many of us stay off the field because we assume we don't have the qualifications to get into the trenches of human brokenness, sin, despair, and injustice. The adversaries are so formidable, and we feel about half the size. But what if I were to tell you that it doesn't matter how many degrees someone has earned, how long a person has pastored, how regularly one is chosen to captain a team or lead a ministry—without paying attention to first things first, that role on the front lines will be rendered ineffective. How we start *matters*. In this section, we focus on our first step. If we don't start well, we will finish poorly. If we don't start well, our evangelistic fears will be confirmed: we are best to stay in our bubble.

So let's turn to our first step. What *is* this news that we call good?

one

AND *YOU* GET *HEAVEN*

"The time has come," he said. "The kingdom of God has come near. Repent and believe the good news!"

—Mark 1:15

The gospel tells us that God is making all things new. He is not only redeeming and restoring people. He is also at work to redeem and restore all of creation. One day everything will be as it was intended to be. That's good news![1]

•————————•

Heard That

When I first met Joseph, I was less than enthusiastic. I was busy. I was doing ministry. My wife and I were serving at a church in Clarksville, Tennessee, and one of my many roles was

---

1. Heather Holleman and Ashley Holleman, *Sent: Living a Life That Invites Others to Jesus* (Chicago: Moody Publishers, 2020), 45.

college pastor. On the day I met Joseph, I was standing outside of a house that was for sale on the edge of Austin Peay State University's campus, considering investing significant finances and time in a home that would serve as both our residence and a college ministry center. We were waiting on our real estate agent, who was a member of our congregation. When our friend pulled up she quickly got out of the car and shot me a look that I wasn't sure how to decipher. Emerging from the other side of the car was Joseph.

Tall, lanky, gaunt, and filthy, Joseph was a sight to behold. His shirt was buttoned about two buttons off, which didn't seem to bother him. His hair went every which way. The front of his clothes were caked with dirt. His shoes were barely holding together. Our friend looked at me and announced, "Pastor Jeff, this is Joseph. He's a new friend of mine. I picked him up on the side of the road on the way here and just felt that you would be the right person to talk to him."

Of course you did, I thought. Internally I was aggravated. I had a busy day and needed to look at this house. It was a big decision for my wife and me. I mean, this was about ministry! Secondly, I thought, *Now he knows where we might live.* But I buried all that down deep, put on my best pastor face, and said, "Of course I can talk with Joseph!"

I invited Joseph into the home we were considering—someone else's home, mind you! I invited him to sit on someone else's couch, and I asked him a few cursory questions. Within minutes, I was in full-blown pastor-evangelist mode, presenting the gospel to a man who looked like he'd just been ridden hard and put away wet by life. What he needed was to get saved! So I explained, you know, that sin separates us from God, that the wages of sin are death, but that God doesn't want anyone to perish, so God in God's good grace—

Interruption. By Joseph. He finished my presentation. After *he* finished, I looked at him and said, "Um, you've heard that one before?"

He slumped his shoulders, gave me a dry smile, and said, "Yeah. A lot." And then he said, "Why is it that Christians always want to get me saved but no one wants to be my friend?"

Ugh. How we start matters. I'd just taken the wrong first step. I'd leapt straight to soul-saving, managing to devalue the whole person, made in the image of God, who bore the name Joseph. My misstep was the result of inadequate theology. I'd botched it. But—praise be to God—Joseph extended far more patience to me than I did to him. I said, "Joseph, I'm sorry. Can I pick you up and take you to lunch this week, just to hang out?"

He said yes.

Destination Disease

Our first steps often proceed from inadequate theology. We often start with, "How might I be saved?" But Jesus seems to start with, "What is the Father up to in this world, and what might that mean to you?" This subtle nuance makes all the difference. Throughout this book I'll introduce you to a few words you may not ever use again, but for the sake of this book they will be helpful.

The first is *soteriology*. This is the question, or the doctrine, of salvation. What does it mean to be saved? How does one become saved? In much of Western Christianity, this is the obsession. We've been told the primary problem is sin. The unfortunate destination is hell. The preferred destination is heaven, and the primary remedy is the grace of Jesus. Tie all of this up into a nice, individualized little bundle, and the whole of Christianity can be boiled down into a personal soul rescue. Salvation is a decision one makes to confess sin and accept grace, thereby guaranteeing a place in heaven. All of this sounds pretty customary, correct? But what if this is the wrong first step? Before you gasp, I'm not saying it doesn't matter—I'm saying perhaps it's not the *first step*.

Instead of starting with "how might I be saved?" Jesus seems to suggest early in his ministry that God is up to something significant in this world, and that something includes you. This something that God is up to, Jesus calls the kingdom of God. This phrase isn't a passing reference but central to everything that comes next. Jesus is kingdom-obsessed. In the Gospel of Mark, Jesus's first sermon—which, to his listeners' delight, is about two sentences!—is, "The time has come. The kingdom of God has come near. Repent and believe the good news!" (1:15). For Jesus, the heart of the good news is the coming of the kingdom of God—which means that the first step for Jesus is not soteriology but *eschatology*, or the doctrine of final things. Eschatology is the concern for God's preferred and final picture of the world and everything in it. It's the aim of God. It's the intentions of God. It's the trajectory toward which all things point. It's the grand declaration that God is up to something in this world, and God will see it come to pass.

Unfortunately, when we talk about eschatology, it often gets muddled in the arguments about end-times theories and fantasized epic battles between good and evil, either preempted by the faithful being sucked out of the world's tumult or rewarded for their perseverance in the great tribulation. Either way, it's more about escape hatches, reading into Revelation images apocalyptic symbols that were never intended, or discerning around which corner the next Antichrist is hiding or which political office they hold. As thrilling as all of that is (not to mention how lucrative a Christian industry such theories have been), it's a tragic, unfortunate misreading of the promise of Jesus throughout his ministry. For Jesus, the promise of God's final things is promised good news. And these final things aren't merely in the far-off distance. They are breaking into the present! Jesus shows up and inaugurates the kingdom, saying, "Pay attention, folks! What God is up to is so close you can almost get your hands on it." The kingdom of God is near!

Throughout the Gospels, the kingdom language emerges as the guiding vision for Jesus's ministry on earth. American Christianity often starts at the point of departure. You get Jesus, and then you get to go somewhere else when you die. But what if what makes the good news so *good* in the twenty-first century is that we don't wait for death? Good news in the form of the kingdom—the redemptive rule and reign of Jesus—is breaking into the present.

From Good to Better

What is this kingdom of which we speak? If we are going to suggest that the first step of evangelism is getting our theology about the kingdom correct, then we should probably dive in and discuss the kingdom. Because I teach university students and have been a pastor for nearly two decades, I've been trained to distill down all our theological verbiage into ideas that make sense. People have little patience for drawn-out, hard-to-understand explanations. What is the kingdom? The kingdom is simply this: The good that God began at creation is the good that God longs to restore. God accomplishes this restoration through the rule and reign of Jesus—begun already, but not fully completed.

At the beginning, the beauty of Genesis is rooted in the worshipful declaration that God makes all things from nothing, orders the chaos, creates time and space, and fills time and space—and it is pronounced "good." Before the beginning of all things became an issue for debates between religion and science, Genesis 1 served as a repetitive liturgy to be read among the worshiping community. We reaffirm that sin was never God's intent for the world or humanity. God makes all things good. God begins with beauty and goodness. *We* introduced the ugly brokenness.

The brilliance of Israel's storytelling in Genesis is that they have the capacity to diagnose the world's issues—and, hence, humanity's proclivity toward rebellion—in about eleven chapters. They know how to get to the heart of what matters. The ugliness and brokenness that ripple out and negatively impact

God's good intentions find their origins in *our* intentional transgression of the created order and our misuse and abuse of one another. This transgression frustrates the harmony of the whole of creation, leaving it, in the apostle Paul's words, "groaning" for redemption (Romans 8:22).

God recommits to the good amid the ugly brokenness. Israel then suggests to us that the God who once declared creation to be good never gave up on the original project. God did not wipe his hands and say, "I gave it a good try, but this is hopeless" (though the Genesis storyteller leaves us wondering if this might not be the outcome of the flood). God recommits, covenanting with creation that the good God intended will be made good again. God is relentlessly tenacious in God's pursuit of the right, good, true, and noble things of creation. Without getting too deep into the woods of the entire biblical story, we can say that God committed to start small in order to go big. God starts with one man's family line that becomes a tribal confederation that becomes a nation that becomes a rag-tag group of peripheral players that becomes a church—with the intention of ultimately redeeming the very ends of the earth. This saving act is consistent with God's original intention that the whole of creation would know of the goodness of God. God has never given up on the good. The same God who once declared creation good longs to say, "That's really, really good!" once again.

Jesus's announcement of the kingdom is in line with God's intentions throughout history. However, Jesus's radical claim is that this season of God's favor—the *eschatological* fullness of time—is beginning now. Eternity is breaking into the present. God's kingdom, first demonstrated in the person of Jesus and to be witnessed in the lives of his followers, is an "on earth as it is in heaven" act of redemption and restoration. This is *really* good news—news worth sharing and celebrating. As Reggie McNeal suggests, "It's time for the people of God to throw a party. A street party. A kingdom party. A party for life, here and now, on earth as it is in heaven. A renewed focus on the kingdom here and now promises help and hope for our communities. It may also halt the church's slide into irrelevance in the eyes of the wider culture."[2] The kingdom of God is the radical space where God gets God's way. At this time, it has already come even though it is not yet fully realized.

The news is good! The kingdom has come! The very aim that God has promised is coming to fruition. Here's where things get *really* good. The kingdom of God is the space where God gets God's way, which means it is a space where the broken are made whole, the left-outs are let in, and the insidious forces of violence and injustice are challenged and toppled. It's the space where the vulnerable are prioritized, the hungry are fed, and the naked are clothed. It's the space where the least, the last, the lost, the weary, the wounded, the bruised, and the broken find healing for their souls. The kingdom is the space where our unchecked egos and unbridled sin are recognized as hopelessly out of sync with God's good melody of creation's intent. The only way to participate in that melody is through repentance and a retuning of your life's instrument to the ways

---

2. Reggie McNeal, *Kingdom Come: Why We Must Give Up Our Obsession with Fixing the Church—and What We Should Do Instead* (Carol Stream, IL: Tyndale, 2015), 17.

of God. The kingdom is the reversal of the world as we know it and all we've become accustomed to. In the kingdom, the first will be last and the last first, the rich are made poor and the poor made rich. The powerful are brought down from their high perches, and the lowly are lifted up. In the kingdom, swords are beaten into plowshares, instruments of death and violence become instruments that cultivate life. In the kingdom, lions lie down with lambs. This is the kingdom of God.

If this is the good news that Jesus sought to both proclaim and embody, you can quickly see why he drew the *types* of crowds he drew. To the forgotten, the ragamuffin, and the spiritual pilgrim—those who had no place in the systems and structures of organized religion and social bias—this news was really good. It meant God hadn't forgotten about them. It meant God had come to set things straight so there would be a place for them—not just in heaven someday, but here and now, on earth as it is in heaven. Of course, the other crowds Jesus drew were those for which this was anything *but* good news. They were the ones who had a lot invested in the world as it was, not as God preferred it—the powerful, the rich, the elite. If Jesus had come with a message that merely pointed to an otherworldly, far-off, someday destination, the latter group might not have cared. However, because Jesus came with the message of a kingdom on earth as it is in heaven, they understood that what he was saying had real-world implications.

The kingdom that Jesus proclaimed is our first step in evangelism. We do not merely go with a message of a "pie-in-the-sky someday hope of heaven beyond the clouds." We go with the revolutionary message that God is up to something in this world, seeking to restore, reclaim, reconcile, and redeem this world to God's intentions and that it's happening *right now.*

And You Get Heaven

So do I get saved?

That might be what you are wondering right now, and the answer is, of course! However, when we start with the right first step, we begin to see that we are saved *for* something and not just saved *from* something (a topic we will return to in chapter 2). When we begin with the assumption that God has never given up on God's pursuit of the good of creation, and humanity has been part of the good becoming bad, it's only natural that God would seek to make good those who made things not so good. God has refused to give up on the whole of creation—which means us! God was not content to turn us over to our sin and the ever-widening chasm of separation it meant for the relationship between God and humanity. God sought to remedy the divide by reconciling us to himself. According to Paul in his letter to the church in Colossae, "But now he has reconciled you by Christ's physical body through death to present you holy in his sight, without blemish and free from accusation" (1:22). God made peace, reconciling himself to us through the blood that Christ shed on the cross.

Jesus embodies not only the kingdom as the preferred picture of God's ultimate purposes, but Jesus also embodies the self-giving, holy love of God. It is a love made vulnerable to human hands, one that suffers under the weight of human sin and evil, a love that felt the lament of victimization and abandonment, a love that—even in the face of the most brutal of deaths—offers for-

And You Get Heaven

giveness, refusing to perpetuate the alienation that has happened between God and humanity. It is a love that suffers the consequence of sin's vicious acts—death. However, it is also a love that will demonstrate its power in refusing to grant death victory over the profound hope of redemption. It is a love that raises the dead to life. Jesus is alive, and as long as Jesus lives, the hope of God's kingdom remains. As Al Tizon notes, "Jesus was the kingdom of God incarnate as he ministered compassion, justice, and forgiveness by word, deed, and miraculous signs, and as he taught the truths and values of the kingdom in ways accessible to the masses. As we know, the forces of darkness tried to snuff out the kingdom by killing Jesus; but death had no ultimate power, as Christ rose on the third day. As long as Jesus is alive, the kingdom is here."[3] And Jesus invites us to transfer our membership from the wrong, perverse, corrupt, idolatrous kingdoms of this world to God's kingdom.

God has made a way through the person of Jesus to shed our allegiance to the world as we have known it and embrace the world as God intended it. This *is* salvation. Salvation isn't a soul escape from the punishment of our obnoxious rebellion— as though Jesus serves our place in timeout so we don't have to. No, salvation is a holistic embrace of a new kingdom that demands our complete allegiance. We follow the Jesus who made a way for us to be included in the good news (and participants—more in chapter 2) of the kingdom of God. Salvation is the means through which God makes possible God's ends for the whole of creation. God is up to something, and God is

---

3. Tizon, *Missional Preaching*, 17.

inviting humanity back into our role in joining God in God's restoration of this world.

Oh—and you get heaven. I will not even attempt an articulate response to all I believe or understand heaven to be. I've literally no idea because I believe eternity with God is a richness and brilliance that leaves me stammering and grasping for words. But I do believe that those who confess their complicity with the rogue kingdoms of this world, repent from their personal participation in the sin that is the bulwark of those rogue kingdoms, receive the grace of forgiveness, and respond to the provision of inclusion will be granted an eternity with God, whatever we imagine that looking like. And that is *also* very good news.

Glimpsing the Kingdom

When we start with, "What is God up to?" and *then* move to, "How might I be saved?" evangelism begins to take on a new expression. No longer are we simply sitting with the Josephs of this world on a stranger's couch, attempting to complete a salvific transaction so we can get on with the rest of our day and feel good that we secured one more name on the roll that will be called up yonder. No, evangelism begins to look different. It becomes obsessed with the kingdom of God and with God's right-making of this world. It takes its time. It doesn't rush to a decision and miss the possibility for relationship. It doesn't cheapen grace by treating it like a drive-by remedy to a life's worth of challenges and struggles. It sits with Joseph and asks the questions, "In what ways is God's kingdom breaking into this moment, this room, into my life and Joseph's life? In what ways can we bear witness to that kingdom in our actions and interactions that demonstrate to this person in front of us God's head-over-heels love for them?" Salvation means, at some level, our participation as good newsers in the kingdom of God, bearing witness to it and pointing at glimpses of it. Salvation that begins with the kingdom assumption means that we are saved by the unmerited grace of God through faith *so that*, as God's handiwork, we can set about to do the things we were originally created to do (see Ephesians 2:8–10).

The Kingdom Shows Up as Friendship

Over the next few months and years, I witnessed the good news of God's kingdom breaking into Joseph's life, and I also witnessed it breaking into our church *through* Joseph's life. I witnessed salvation. At first, it started with a series of lunches at Arby's. During that time, I learned Joseph's story. As someone who struggled with bipolar schizophrenia, he'd spent the better part of his teenage and early adult years shuffling through agencies who only knew him as a case number. He'd been abused on more than one occasion. He'd lived in a tent for seven years. His list of struggles went on and on.

I started picking him up for church on Wednesday nights and Sunday mornings. To go to church with the preacher means you are there before everyone else and don't leave until after everyone else. It also meant I put him to work. He helped me set up and tear down, always a bit disheveled, his hair always unkempt. He went to Sunday school with me and started to befriend class members. For a young man who was used to life on his own, he now had several people reaching out to him, taking him to lunch, inviting him to their homes to do odd jobs. The kingdom was breaking into his life. In the beginning he did swindle a person or two. Our attachments to old kingdoms die hard, and transference to God's kingdom means that old habits and survival tactics also die hard. We had to correct him from time to time. There were times when he'd have a mental break and end up in the hospital for a few days. Good newsers would care for him and visit him. The kingdom of God was breaking in.

I remember the day Joseph came bounding into my office with a brand-new haircut. One of the good-newser ladies in the congregation who owned a salon had cut his hair for free. The kingdom of God was breaking in.

I remember the day when he, exhausted by his never-ending pain from rotten teeth, came into my office and shared that the good-newser dentist in the church had offered to pull all his teeth and fit him with dentures for free. The kingdom of God was breaking in.

I remember the day he and I sat worshiping together at a community worship service. He was the only friend of mine who was willing to go with me. We sat together and cared for my two little boys, and the kingdom of God was breaking in.

Joseph became one of our primary greeters at the church, he was baptized, he earned his GED with the help of good-newser congregants, he got into college, and he eventually got married. The kingdom of God was breaking in. Salvation had come to Joseph's life in a holistic and beautifully redemptive way.

Two specific instances stand out to me. One evening, on our way home from church, I asked him, "Joseph, how are you doing—really?"

He said, "Jeff, you know my bipolar schizophrenia. Well, since I've started coming to this church, the highs aren't as high any longer, and the lows are not nearly as low. I know that I'm never alone."

The kingdom of God had broken in and become good news to him. He was experiencing the salvation of Jesus.

A couple months later, I was in a hurry on a Sunday morning, trying to navigate the sea of people between our two full services. There was a single hallway through which people moved to the sanctuary, and it was packed. Amid all those people, I heard a loud (and, let's be honest, obnoxious) voice above the din: "Pastor Jeff, you know what?"

I saw Joseph at the opposite end of the hallway, and I also saw that now everyone was looking at us.

I fired back, "What, Joseph?"

He said, "I've got more friends in this church than you do!" And he was right. He did. And the good news of Jesus had come through his life to others. Joseph had become a good newser.

The story of Joseph reminds me of the story of the bleeding woman in Mark 5. Having been separated and alienated from community, companionship, and redemptive care because of her perceived unacceptability, she in desperation reached out to grab the hem of Jesus's garment. Jesus "realized that power had gone out from him," and he found this woman, "trembling with fear" (v. 30, 33). Jesus told her, "Daughter, your faith has healed you. Go in peace and be freed from your suffering" (v. 34). The word for "healed" in the Greek is the same word we often translate as "salvation." Her desperate faith saved, healed, and made her whole. It returned her to community as a representative of Jesus's goodness. In desperation, Joseph grabbed hold of the hem of Jesus's garment—otherwise known as the church—and was saved, healed, made whole, and sent back into the community as a witness to good news.

The kingdom of God broke into Joseph's life, into my life, and into the church. Joseph experienced salvation and became a participant in the good news of God's kingdom as a recipient of that same good news. None of it happened quickly, but the fruitfulness of God's good making of the world is rarely ready-made. Instead, it is the steady process of doing the work necessary to demonstrate faithfully the good news of God's kingdom so that others might be saved.

two

DO *WORK*

For we are God's handiwork, created in Christ Jesus to do good works, which God prepared in advance for us to do.
                                                    —Ephesians 2:10

Our work—not just our employment but all aspects of human culture—can be a preview of what the fullness of the kingdom will be like. We don't build the kingdom; that job is exclusively reserved for God. But we can live in such a way that our lives provide a glimpse of what the kingdom of God will be like.[1]

A Disenchanted World

As I sat with my friend at a coffee shop, we chatted about the kind of work we were up to. I'm a college professor who generally teaches the intersection of religion and culture, dabbling in all of the things we are told not to talk about: politics, economics, religion, race, justice—all of that stuff that's easy to talk

---

1. Goheen and Mullins, *The Symphony of Mission*, 85.

about! She is a contract lawyer with Ivy League degrees who worked in Washington, DC. She's a high-caliber leader and a genuinely great person. She comes from what I would call the highly secularized urban environment that is common to the twenty-first century. Faith isn't part of her everyday vocabulary. Though not particularly drawn to the things of faith, she is a good friend of mine and cares deeply about what I do.

She asked, "What are you working on?" I was prepping to teach a class on racial reconciliation and trying to figure out how to navigate the absurdity of being a middle-aged white man teaching racial reconciliation at a predominantly white school to a majority-white class.

She said, "I'm jealous. Jeff, I see what you do and I think, *That matters*. Then I look at what I do. I get paid a ridiculous amount of money to do what I do—I mean, *ridiculous*. And I'm good at it. But every day I wonder, *Does any of this really matter? Am I making a difference?*" I could see the concern in her eyes.

This is emblematic of the challenges we face as Christians in the society in which we live. We live in an increasingly post-Christian context in the West. There was a time in the nostalgic past when faith and Christianity held a cultural place among many people in the United States. However, the assumption of Christendom has eroded over the last few decades, for many reasons that we will resist trying to parse here. As Christianity has waned, secularism has waxed. The word "secular" is a very broad word that can mean a number of things. In many church circles, it simply means "non-church-related stuff." We have Christian universities and secular universities. What I'm talking about is more than churchy distinctions. Secularism and secularization are the natural outgrowths of a Christianity that held more sway culturally than it did confessionally. In the U.S., people identified as Christians because of where they lived and maybe because they also believed in God. What wasn't always as robust was a confessional faith, an understanding that "I've become part of a new kingdom with a new Lord, and his name is Jesus."

Throughout the mid-to-late twentieth century—again, for a lot of cultural reasons (not all of which can be pinned on the shoulders of elite academics and Democrats)—faith gave way to the rise of "nones," people who had no religious affiliation. Religious faith, and especially Christianity, no longer exercised the same kind of influence on people's imaginations and worldviews. They were now constructing worldviews devoid of concern for God. This is a radical moment in the history of humanity. For far longer than this current moment in history, the world was assumed to be enchanted, filled with gods and demons, angels and specters. Humanity attributed what it didn't know to the supernatural. With the advent of modern science within the last 350 years and the ability to explain the unexplainable, religious faith didn't lose its position overnight. Even if science could demystify the world, religion was still a solid force for social mooring and personal morality. However, even that began to give way, and slowly the world became increasingly disenchanted.

Secularism is the intentional process of emptying the world of transcendence (supernatural categories beyond us that can't be explained by us) in favor of radical immanence (what we can taste, touch, feel, experience, observe, and explain). God, heaven, and hell became relics of an ancient past, and were unnecessary for modern life. Many of our urban settings, and increasingly our suburban and even rural areas, are becoming post-Christian and increasingly secular. Cue the alarmists. But wait! What if this is an opportunity and not a threat for the church? What if we start with the right first step and then move to the second?

Many in the church—especially those who are committed to evangelism—suggest that we merely need to get more people saved. Great! But the problem is that they start in the wrong place. They want to start with heaven and hell—categories that secularists are unconcerned with. Secularists aren't angry at God or scared of hell. God's simply not on their on radar. My friend wrestling with her career choice wasn't struggling with questions of heaven and hell and what we call salvation. She was wrestling with *meaning* and *purpose* because those made sense to her. However, I would say she *was* wrestling with salvation even though she didn't have the words for it. Here's the gift of starting in the right place.

Do Work

When I coached high school football, I had a quirky, fun, and at times ridiculously obnoxious group of students. They were great, and I loved every one of them. One of my favorites was a young man named Bubba. I coached football in the American South. It's a requisite you have at least one student or coach on the team called Bubba. Bubba was an undersized linebacker, hard as nails, and an even harder worker. Before practice and all the games he'd run through the locker room, flex his biceps, and say, "Do work son!" in the faces of his teammates. This was his announcement that it was game time. They had work to do!

I've held on to this statement and, oddly enough, believe it applies to the good news of the gospel. Too often, when we talk about the gospel, our obsession with starting with departure and destination leaves us with a transactional faith that is more concerned with life after death than with life itself—which is unfortunate because Jesus himself says very clearly, "I came that they may have life and have it abundantly" (John 10:10, NRSVUE). Somewhere along the way, the idea of abundant life here on earth, as promised by Jesus, was lost in the American escapist theological preoccupation with the destination of heaven. Although we cannot earn our way to heaven, doing the work of God mustn't ever be completely disconnected from our salvation. Participating in the mission of God ("doing work") may not earn us our salvation, but it is central nonetheless.

If we assume that God is up to something in this world and that God is restoring this world to God's original intent, and if we believe that part of that plan is to invite humanity to join God in that work, then our experience of salvation must have something to do with reclaiming and embodying the good purposes for which we are created. So what we do—our purpose—must be tied up in our salvation. God creates humanity as co-laborers in his good making of the world. We abandoned our role, but God never abandoned us. When God saves us, he is conscripting us back into that work. This means that the unique craftsmanship of God, which is each of our lives, positions us in some way as unique contributors in God's good making of the world. What my friend was asking was, "How might I be saved?"—not *from* some pit of fire but *for* a meaningful sense of purpose. God created her to do good work.

Words Matter

There are many evangelistic words and phrases surrounding salvation that make me uncomfortable. Among them are "soul-winning," "depopulating hell," "winning people to heaven," and the list goes on. Each of these words and phrases has its origin in a unique cultural setting where there was a time when maybe they made sense. I would never question the sincerity of the people who use them or the passion with which they pursue those who are disconnected from Jesus. That doesn't make me any more comfortable with those words. I prefer words like "apprenticing Jesus," "kingdom-recruiting," or "saying yes to being a follower of Jesus." These words are less passive and more active. They seem to demonstrate the biblical reality that salvation is caught up in active pursuit of Jesus and participation in the kingdom of God. When I look at the life of Jesus, I rarely see, *Hey, stand over there—I've got this.* Instead, I more often see, *Hey, follow me, and I will show you how to fish for people. Follow me because you've got some good work to do.*

Starting at the kingdom and God's good making of the world inclines us to see everyone we come into contact with as potential *recipients* of and *participants* in God's good making in the world. We see them in their beauty, which is often masked and buried under wounds, shame, idolatrous pursuits, ego, and many other layers of untapped kingdom potential. Instead of starting with the assumption that this person is headed to one of two places—and quickly—and I need to do my part—quickly!—to secure the right destination for them, we see people less as salvation projects and more as beautifully crafted masterpieces who need to be shown how to see themselves in the same light as God sees them. We recognize that, in calling Peter and Andrew, Jesus was calling them into purpose prior to promising them a destination. When calling Paul, Jesus was calling him into a purpose prior to promising him a destination. They were being called to be participants in the glorious design of God's redemptive kingdom. Jesus was recruiting them, *inviting* them into good work and thereby into their salvation.

What if evangelists—rather than concerning ourselves with the specific actions of winning souls and taking names—began to recognize evangelism itself as the life of a good newser who strolls alongside others, demonstrates faithfully the good news, cares compassionately and empathetically for every person we come into contact with, reminds them they are beautifully created masterpieces, and recruits them to join us in our Jesus-following as we discover the unique role we have to play in what God is up to in this world?

What Called You Forth?

Emily came bounding into the coffee shop. She was one of the former baristas I'd not seen in months due to both COVID and a change of occupation. When she saw me, she lit up as if she had some good news. She sat down to catch up, and soon I found out she was moving from Chicago to the Big Apple in pursuit of a master's degree in education.

When I met Emily, I was impressed. She was twenty-two years old, fresh out of college, working at the coffee shop in a brand-new city, trying to find her way and figure things out. She was bubbly, fun, kind, funny, and genuinely interested in others. She reminded me of most of the college students I taught. A few months back, she had told me she was quitting her job at the coffee shop to pursue a long-term substitute-teaching position at a school, something that promised more consistent hours and better pay. I celebrated with her and then didn't see her for months. Emily is not someone I've witnessed demonstrate a keen interest in things of faith, but when I've been with Emily, I have seen God's craftsmanship in her, even if she doesn't.

The day she told me she was leaving Chicago to pursue her master's degree in education, she said to me, "Jeff, when I was in that classroom, it hit me. This is what I'm meant to do. I *want* to do this."

Knowing she didn't have the language for describing a "calling" and God's purposes, I said to her, "You had your called-forth moment."

She looked genuinely puzzled.

I explained, "A few months ago I was reading in a book called *Becoming Brave*, by Brenda Salter McNeil, about a Ghanaian concept from the Akan people. When they want to know someone better, they ask, 'What called you forth?'" This is how Salter McNeil writes it:

In asking that question they are essentially asking the person to discuss why they believe they were born. Perhaps the name they were given by their parents holds some insight into what they view as their purpose in life. By asking, "What called you forth?" they are really interested in knowing, *Why did God cause you to be born at this time in history? Do you know your purpose for being on the planet? What is happening in the world today that called you forth?*[2]

I told Emily, "When you were in that classroom, it was your 'What called you forth?' moment. You are tapping into that unique thing you've been created to do."

She said, "I'm getting goosebumps, and I'm going to cry. Yes! That's exactly what it felt like to me."

We hugged, and she left. And I had just evangelized. No, she didn't pray the sinner's prayer right there. I was planting, not harvesting. But she was nudged to realize she's a person who has a purpose. She knows who I am and what I believe, and I know she knows I believe in her. I genuinely pray and hope that, at some point, she connects that sense of purpose with the point of origin of her purpose and becomes an apprentice of Jesus. In the meantime, she's reclaiming the person God created her to be.

When I meet people in my neighborhood, when I sit with friends in the coffee shop, when I meet with students in my office, when I host my men's small group Bible Study on

---

2. Brenda Salter McNeil, *Becoming Brave: Finding the Courage to Pursue Racial Justice Now* (Grand Rapids: Brazos Press, 2020), 51.

Zoom—I want to know: What's called you forth? What is the unique role you were created to fulfill in the work of God's kingdom and his good-making of this world?

Do Good Work

As I sat with my friend, I felt the weight of her question: "I wonder if what I do matters at all?" From my perspective, she wasn't having an existential problem or an early midlife crisis. I saw her question as theological. *Do I believe there is anything about my life that is unique enough to impact this world in a good and meaningful way? In what ways do I matter? How might I be saved for . . . ?* When I look at my friend, I see a treasure trove of untapped kingdom potential. I see a person who is endowed with gifts that God could leverage in significant ways to impact the lives of those around her. I see a woman who might remain a contract lawyer in commercial real estate but who *could* leverage her intelligence, kindness, deep knowledge of Chicago, and finances to make an immense difference. I long to journey with her in connecting herself to a sense of purpose—which, oddly enough, often results in connecting to the origin of that purpose.

The power of seeing evangelism as recruitment into the kingdom and recognizing kingdom purpose in what we do is that it endows every person with a real sense of significance. We aren't just muddling our way through life. We aren't just trying to get by. We aren't just moving from one thing to the next, from one workweek to the next. No, as kingdom participants who are engaged in the good-making of this world, everything we do at work, at home, or at play has kingdom significance.

When we embrace the good news of the kingdom, we begin to realize we are being recruited into something *on* earth rather than waiting for something *after* earth. This shift means that the whole of what we do—every job we work, every word we speak, every relationship we are in—is endowed with significance and purpose. In the twenty-first century, a time when many struggle against the monotonous meaninglessness and despair of a secularized world, recruiting people into kingdom participation can offer renewed hope for life.

three
LEAVING THE *"GOOD"* OUT OF THE *GOOD NEWS*

I am astonished that you are so quickly deserting the one who called you to live in the grace of Christ and are turning to a different gospel—which is really no gospel at all. Evidently some people are throwing you into confusion and are trying to pervert the gospel of Christ.

—Galatians 1:6–7

But how sad so few individuals equally committed to Jesus Christ ever became part of the movement. For what all that political activity needed—and lacked—was spiritual input. Even now, I do not understand why so many evangelicals find a sense of commitment to civil rights and to Jesus Christ an either-or proposition. One of the greatest tragedies of the civil rights movement is that evangelicals surrendered their leadership in the movement by default to those with bankrupt theology or no theology at all, simply because the vast majority of Bible-believing Christians ignored a great and crucial opportunity in history for genuine ethical action. The evangelical church—whose basic theology is the same as mine—had not gone on to preach the whole gospel.[1]

Toby Keith on Sunday Morning

"Shouldn't we at least acknowledge that all this 'this-is-a-Christian-nation' stuff happened at the expense of indigenous peoples having their lands taken from them and Africans enslaved by their 'Christian' masters? I'm confused—wouldn't it be good to at least acknowledge it's not as nice and tidy as we make it seem?"

These were the words of a young woman who was brand new to both the faith and to our church. She had just attended one of our large community outreach events, and she was genuinely both irritated and confused. We had attempted a large outreach event, wanting to meet people where they were by having a First Responders and Veterans Sunday. We were pastoring in a military town, so it felt like it made sense in our planning meeting. We wanted to eliminate any obstacle that might get in the way of people coming to church, so we held the event at the local high school instead of the church. Our evangelical zeal brought us visions of floods of people coming to the altars to be saved.

---

1. John M. Perkins, *Let Justice Roll Down* (Grand Rapids: Baker Books, 2014).

What unfolded was a bit different than what we had in mind. We invited first responders, veterans, politicians, and military brass. Different people spoke throughout the morning, and the music had more the feel of a rousing Fourth of July parade than it did a worship service. An unedited video from a military spokesperson had a song about putting a boot up Saddam's—well, you can guess. One guest speaker, a Twin Towers survivor from 9/11, gave a rousing Christian nationalist manifesto. At one point in the service, I felt like I needed to take a shower. But the young woman who was brand new to the faith hit me the hardest. She could not conceivably reconcile what she'd been hearing at church with what she had just witnessed and heard in the high school, at an event put on by the same church she had been attending for the last few weeks, and an event I had a substantial role in pulling off. She couldn't reconcile the message of Jesus with the Christian propaganda she'd just heard. She voiced her concern, and we never saw her again.

This story illustrates one thing: the good news is only good if it's good.

Notch on the Belt

I think I might have become nauseated the first time I heard the term "close the deal" during an evangelism training. I was fairly new to Christianity and still a bit skeptical of these church people I'd become intertwined with. Yet I'd experienced the redemptive power of good news and had an earnest desire to become a good newser to others. Evangelism training seemed like the appropriate next step for me, and I don't for one instant doubt the sincerity of those leading the training. Under the theological framework they had adopted, some of what they said made sense. If people are perilously headed toward hell and you are the only thing standing between them and the lake of fire and you legitimately don't know if they might leave that coffee shop and get killed on the way home, only to be lost forever, the urgency of closing the deal makes a certain amount of sense. But I couldn't square that urgency with the invitation into relationship and the patience that Jesus himself seemed to exercise in Scripture. Likewise, we learned tactics and strategies for how to turn a conversation toward spiritual things, cut through hesitation, present the gospel clearly and concisely according to one of about four methods, and force a moment of decision. All of it felt highly tactical and not fully genuine to me. But who was I to say? I was new.

So I swallowed my concerns, and I got good at the evangelism method I was taught. I adopted the same sincerity and misguided urgency. It always felt a bit forced, but I was notching the belt. I was "leading people to Jesus," "winning souls," and "getting people saved." God even used some of that—boy, am I thankful for his grace! Over time, I realized I was learning how to manipulate conversations, listen without empathizing, awkwardly insert my story to turn attention toward testimony, and get people to buy into something they didn't fully understand. At the end of the day, I got credit. I'll never forget the time I *didn't* get credit—a young man told me he'd just surrendered his life to Jesus and that it was transformative. I sulked. I had led him to Jesus *weeks* earlier, and now someone else was getting credit! I shouldn't have been surprised; my explanation of the gospel had been woefully inadequate for someone with the brokenness this young man had experienced. It needed time to simmer. He was reckoning with the cost and hadn't been ready yet when I spoke to him.

We are not messengers of the good news when we treat people as trophies, numbers, recipients of canned presentations that lack the depth and sincerity their unique lives and journeys deserve. As Dave and Jon Ferguson note, "Your friends and neighbors are not projects; they are people."[2] I'm not saying we ought not use *any* tools as someone makes a commitment to Jesus. I'm saying that when we deploy those tools in manipulative fashion, we do more harm than good. Good news is only good when it's born of sincerity of connection, compassion of heart, patience of listening, and the willingness to journey well and long with a person in relationship. It doesn't carry the air of a divine pyramid scheme or a used-car salesperson. It's good when the person sharing that good news is willing to be a friend, to love and listen well. It's good when a person feels woven into the fabric of relationship, given safe space to explore, question, and doubt without pressure to decide before they've taken time to discover the recognition that the decision to follow is more than a prayer; it is a conscious decision to leave behind one way of life and adopt a new way of living. It is not and *should not* be an easy decision.

---

2. Dave Ferguson and Jon Ferguson, *BLESS: 5 Everyday Ways to Love your Neighbor and Change the World* (Washington, DC: Salem Books, 2021), 9.

Who Is My Neighbor?

In the Parable of the Prodigal Son, the father is described as irrationally, irresponsibly, illogically, scandalously inclusive—indiscriminate with his love. We tend to focus on the son, but the father's character is the point of the parable. The father loves against all odds. He *chooses* to love those whom he has every right to forsake. The father refuses to take a posture of self-justified, self-righteous distance. The father recognizes that the absence of any of his children is a loss for him. Oh, to take our cues from such a story! To begin our pursuit of good newsing and evangelism from a posture of that kind of love!

Unfortunately, too often the church begins with the wrong story, with attempting to determine who is worthy of God's care and concern: *Who is my neighbor?* This question is born of another posture in the church that has often stripped the church of the goodness of its news—the desire to classify and categorize people based on assumed measures of acceptability. We are most inclined to find ourselves responsible to those who are already the most like us. Entirely homogenous churches spring up, where those pursued are already those who will be the easiest to assimilate, those who are only a little dollop of Jesus away from fitting into our holy huddle. We love those who are like us, and we fear, ignore, dismiss, and pass off those who are most like the proverbial "them."

I'll never forget the staff meeting when my pastor came in, shaken. He had received a call from another pastor in the community, describing a woman who had sought to be part of their church. His question to my pastor was, "Do you think you could take her? I heard you take her kind."

This is not good news. When people don't pass the church's litmus test of what makes them worthy or acceptable for concern and care—whether because of their background, ethnicity, financial status, mental health, disability, sexual orientation, or any other range of easily excluding factors—they will not hear any goodness in our news. When we adopt an us-them mentality, determining who *qualifies* for neighborly care, we've already stripped the news of all its goodness—not to mention this behavior is absolutely at odds with nearly every message of Jesus in the Scriptures, messages that consistently suggest there is no "us" and no "them" but only a collective *all of us* in pursuit of God—broken, imperfect, incomplete beggars in search of the bread of life, teaching and telling other beggars where they too can get food. Only when the work of evangelism is scandalously inclusive and indiscriminate in its love and care—going into the highways and byways to make known the good news of Jesus among the left-outs, the disregarded, and the easily dismissed—will it ever be good news.

A Plague of Prosperity

"What—does Jesus not like rich people?"

This was the question I received at our early-morning men's group. I had warned the guys—guys I'd been in relationship with for over a year—that this next section of Luke would not sit well. We had arrived at Luke's version of Matthew's Sermon on the Mount, known as the Sermon on the Plain.

In the Sermon on the Plain in Luke, Jesus is a bit more prickly. Instead of saying, "Blessed are the poor in spirit" (Matthew 5:3), he says simply, "Blessed are you who are poor" (Luke 6:20). Later he says, "Woe to you who are rich" (Luke 6:24).

I explained to the men in my group that Jesus had a tenuous relationship with wealth. They were committed Jesus apprentices, but something didn't square with them. We have been taught that our riches are a sign of God's blessing. So how could Jesus be condemning the very thing that God's favor and blessing provided?

The problem we face in the West is our wealth and luxury. The U.S. American experiment has provided levels of wealth and comfort to more people than has ever been known throughout history. Because the message of the United States has been that we are a "Christian nation," many have assumed that this country's prosperity is God's blessing. God's favor then becomes woven into the fabric of wealth. Normally this would simply be something that preachers would have to debunk from the pulpit, reminding people that following Jesus doesn't guarantee wealth, health, or prosperity. Christians are as likely as anyone else in the world to experience grief, suffering, financial struggles, illness, and other hardships. The Christian message is that God is faithful *in and through* all trials. But what happens when an entire counter-theology emerges to baptize this insidious allure of wealth—touted by convincing propagandists who style themselves as Christian preachers—is what is known as the "prosperity gospel."

To be unequivocally clear: the prosperity gospel is no gospel at all. It is a perversion of the Christian message, a co-opted and corrupted collection of carefully chosen, cherry-picked verses that bears no resemblance to the life, mission, ministry, and message of Jesus. The good news of the kingdom is not embedded in the United States American dream of extravagant wealth, material possession, or the deranged transformation of the God of love into a cosmic vending machine whereby, if we dial in the right prayer and pull the knob, we will get what our faith claims.

Many people I come across seem to carry with them the assumption that what they see on TV and the lavish extravagance of a select group of so-called Christian leaders is what Christianity is supposed to be about. This well-marketed perversion is so loud that it often threatens to drown out the quiet voices of faithful, sacrificial, authentic Jesus followers. We do not bring good news when we attempt a sinful blend (called *syncretism*) of the values of this world with the values of God's kingdom. Remember, what makes God's kingdom such good news is that it is an *alternative* to the world. The poor didn't follow Jesus because he promised to take away the struggle and strain of daily life; they followed him because he included them in the long game of redemption, promising them the strength to endure, the favor to know they are loved, and the consistency of his presence.

People who measure God's faithfulness by their circumstances often find themselves let down. Living as a kingdom participant is not about bending the Lord's will to meet our needs but allowing the Lord to bend our will to meet his mission. The propagators of prosperity-gospel theology prey upon people's vulnerabilities, fears, and selfish desires, none of which is consistent with the ministry and life of Jesus.

How did I answer the question in my small group about Jesus and rich people? "Yes, Jesus loves rich people. But you need to understand that the wealth you've been given is less a demonstration of unique favor from God and more of a unique responsibility that God has called you to steward. That's what makes this apprenticing-Jesus thing so difficult. We have to act in alignment with God's call."

A History of Unseemly Behavior

The good news is only good if it's good! And it only becomes good if we can confess when we've turned the good into the not-so-good. This confession is the recognition that, as Christians, we have an unfortunate history of unseemly behavior.

One day I was sitting with my friend and his wife at the coffee shop, chatting and having breakfast. We had known this couple for about six months, had been to their house, and were preparing to share Thanksgiving dinner with them. She has a faith background but doesn't currently practice. He is Jewish by ethnicity and atheist by confession. During the breakfast, she asked me, "Jeff, what's it like teaching at an evangelical university?"

Record-scratch moment. Her husband's head had been down, chomping away on his croissant. When his wife asked this question, he looked me in the eye and said, "You're an evangelical." I understood this flat statement to mean, *You've got some explaining to do.* Of course, he knew what I did for a living and where I did it, but he had never made the connection about evangelicalism. For him, that was a loaded word, as it is for many people. For someone who is ethnically Jewish, the word "evangelicalism" may bring up the long, painful, and often violent history of anti-Semitism that has plagued Christianity. Christianity has often been wrapped in imperialist, nationalist, supremacist garb, leaving in its wake many broken, bruised, and battered lives. I could understand why my association with evangelicalism wouldn't immediately earn me any points with my friend.

Christianity—especially Western, imperialistic, colonizing Christianity—has much it needs to recognize as deterrents to faith. Christianity has both historically and recently endorsed positions of taking land away from indigenous people groups, slavery, racist policies and practices, anti-intellectualism, anti-Semitism, anti-immigration, fear of "the other," pro-war, and pro-nation. When Christians and especially Christian leaders take these positions that appear to be in conflict with the ministry and message of Jesus, people tend to step back and ask, *What is the real message of Christianity?* And they are not wrong to ask that question. How can a movement that was initiated by a poor carpenter in ancient Israel—a movement that birthed a marginalized community of people with little to no clout or political influence and who operated under the assumptions of vulnerability and nonviolence—turn into a movement that gives rise to violence, abuse, and a pathological dualism that turns all "others" into threats to be converted, subordinated, or killed?

People know history. People understand that this so-called Christian nation came at the expense of stealing land from indigenous populations who were then sequestered on reservations, only for the U.S. government to break treaty after treaty after treaty with them. People know that, as urban demographics began to shift—due in large part to socially sponsored segregation and racist agendas—churches participated in the "white flight" that removed them from those environments and into the suburbs, giving birth to a form of Christianity that is disconnected from the plight of the poor. People know the long history of religiously sanctioned misogyny that continues to subordinate women and silence victims of abuse in the church. People understand the sordid history, and they demand confession and repentance—a commitment to right the wrongs that Christianity has perpetrated and been complicit in. It's not good news when it looks like that!

This Is Why We Can't Have Nice Things

"Is there any way to do this Jesus thing without all the dogma and drama?"

A good friend asked me this question as we walked through the neighborhood, drinking coffee and spending time together. We had just emerged from the January 6 insurrection at the Capitol. My friend is an incredible guy with an affinity toward religion but no confessional faith.

As we walked, he said, "As I watched all that stuff unfold at the Capitol, I saw the Christian symbols, and I've heard about some of the statements key pastors have made. It seems pretty messy. Internally, do you ever talk about those things?"

I laughed. If he only *knew* how often we talk about those things internally!

My friend was pointing to the challenges of Christianity and politics and the ways that especially evangelical Christians are recognized in the United States as a strategic voting bloc—with pundits, platforms, and politicians that seem to consistently tout a worldview that is really problematic for people wondering, *How exactly do you square that with Jesus?*

Said another way, every four years Christianity is decidedly *not* good news for a lot of marginalized populations in the U.S. That wording may seem harsh, but I believe it is fair. I've pastored three churches through a number of election cycles and taught at a university during one. I've experienced just how contentious, divisive, and incendiary politics can be in the church. I've been the recipient of both veiled and overt threats and diatribes because I have refused to endorse someone's passionate belief that their politics are the only Christian politics. Churches divide over politician support or along party lines. Jesus becomes St. Republican or St. Democrat.

Instead of the church living in this uneasy tension as citizens of the kingdom of God (the good news), the church—to its own detriment—has often conflated party politics with the way of Jesus. But worldly politics are *not* the way of Jesus. As much as we may believe passionately in our political postures, worldly politics are not the primary way the world will be made good again. They are only a tool through which *some* good things can be achieved. As much trust and hope as I may have in my chosen candidate, I'm definitely not looking for a Messiah figure

to make all our social ills disappear. All of politics is fraught
with perversion. All politicians are sinners in need of grace. All
platforms are imperfect and incomplete. All nations are finite.
All pomp and circumstance is propaganda. As Christians, we
are meant to be strangers and aliens in this world. We are supposed to live in the tension between allegiance to the kingdom
of God and our obligations to the kingdoms of this world. When
we become the uncritical mouthpiece of any party, or the religious arm of endorsement for any politician, we are in imminent
danger of losing the goodness of our message. We turn "God
and country" into "god *as* country." This is not good news.

As I walked with my friend, I explained the history of Christianity's complicity with perverse politics and the spiritual gymnas-
tics we've been guilty of to justify our unholy alliances. I spoke
about the kingdom of God. I said the word "gospel."

He asked, "What's this 'gospel' word you keep mentioning?"

I had the privilege of sharing what I believe about Jesus and the
kingdom of God.

That's when he asked, "Is there a way to follow Jesus without
all the dogma and drama?"

I responded, "I sure hope so! Jesus invited us to believe that he
is the Way, the Truth, and the Life. I believe the Jesus way of
living is truly the best way of living. I hope that means I can do
it without participating in the antics that give Christians a bad
name. To do that, I have to commit to being a witness to the
kingdom."

My friend and I have had more conversations about it since that walk. He's still on the way, but he's closer than he realizes to saying yes to apprenticing Jesus.

SECTION 2
Working the Soil

But the seed falling on good soil refers to someone who hears the word and understands it. This is the one who produces a crop, yielding a hundred, sixty or thirty times what was sown.
—Matthew 13:23

We have neglected the truth that a good farmer is a craftsman of the highest order, a kind of artist.[1]

●·······················●

Planting Gardens

There is something about growing your own food. I don't know if it's an evolutionary throwback to our hunter-gatherer days, if it's a sense of empowerment through self-sustainability, or if it's just the beauty of watching life unfold before our very eyes. There's just something about growing your own food. I'm inclined to believe it has something to do with our spiritual

---

1. Wendell Berry, *The Gift of Good Land: Further Essays, Cultural and Agricultural* (New York: North Point Press, 1981).

hardwiring. In Genesis we are commanded to steward the earth, to cultivate life—a harmony that was supposed to exist between humanity and the earthy substance of the created order. When sin enters the story, this harmony is frustrated, and humans are left to tend to the earth with the sweat of our brow, even as it produces thorns and thistles. But cultivating the soil—sinking our hands down deep into the dirt, feeling the soil between our fingers, and tending to fledgling plants—is somewhere in our spiritual hardwiring.

My wife, Angie, and I have owned a couple of houses and lived in many more. In each of the two we owned, we wanted to give ourselves to the work of planting a garden. Neither of us has a particularly green thumb, but we had a desire, a willingness to work, and an eagerness to learn. I wish I could tell you there was already a tilled, prepared, ready-to-plant plot of land at each house where we tried, but that wasn't the case in either place. At both homes, we looked out onto our lawn and had to envision gardens where there were none. In the case of our first house, all we had was a poorly sunlit area along the side of the house on a steep downward slope. In the second house, we had an acre of mostly downward-sloping land. There was a small, level spot along the side of our outbuilding. In both places, all there was where we wanted gardens was grass.

At the first house, I set out to establish a garden. First, I had to dig out a level piece in the downward slope. On the back end of the garden, that meant digging down about twenty-four inches to bring it even with the lowest point, skimming the grass from the top, and being introduced to Tennessee clay and gigantic rocks. It was hard work. With only a shovel and a pickaxe, I worked the

soil. I turned the soil. I shifted the soil from one spot to the other.
I had to build a retaining wall along the backside of the garden
to keep the side of the hill from collapsing on the plants during a
hard rain. And did I mention the rocks? Far too many times, my
teeth rattled and my hands quaked as I struck boulders buried
deep in the earth. Once all that was finished, I realized I needed to
condition the soil. There was too much clay. I had to haul in dirt to
turn in and create a plot conducive for growth. It needed nutrients
and defenses against rabbits and deer. After a late winter and early
spring of work, it was ready for planting. That year we had a mea-
ger harvest of a few tomatoes, peppers, and cucumbers in a plot of
land that took way too long to prepare.

At the second house, I had a tiller. I knew, from what I learned
the first time around, that this plot of land would need a good
year before it was ready for planting. I staked the edges of where
I wanted to put the garden and set out with the tiller. It drove
its spikes deep into the ground, tearing up the sod, revealing
well-saturated soil that was dark and rich—and full of rocks. So
many rocks! On multiple occasions I had to stop the tiller, grab a
hammer, and beat rocks out from where they had become lodged
between the blades. There were so many rocks that I made a
practice of going out every few weeks after a hard rain and
chucking them out from the plot of land. I conditioned the soil,
added some lime, fertilized, and let the plot sit fallow the first
summer. The next spring, I tilled and weeded until I had just the
plot I wanted. Then we planted, and it grew and grew and grew.
We had more cucumbers, zucchini, watermelon, peppers, and
tomatoes than we knew what to do with. We couldn't give them
away fast enough.

In both cases, there was no garden to start with. We had to crack the earth, do the work, till the soil, condition the soil, and prepare it for the planting. Regardless of the yield—whether little or much—it was worth it. There's just something about growing your own food. I think it's in our spiritual wiring. I wonder if that's why farming and gardening images are used so often in Scripture. Jesus consistently points to the work of farmers and says things like, "The kingdom of God is like . . ."

When a Parable Becomes a Copout

"I think it's too easy," I said from the back of the room.

Sometimes I think the Lord likes to have a little fun with me. I was feeling persnickety, and twice in consecutive weeks at two denominational gatherings, leaders had referenced the Parable of the Sower. Many of us know the parable. The farmer went out and started pitching seed. Some fell on the path, and birds came and ate it. Some fell among the rocks, and though they sprung up quickly they lacked roots and so could not live. Some fell on what was apparently good ground, only to have weeds spring up and choke the life out of it. Finally, some fell on good soil, yielding abundance. Of course, the encouragement many take away from this parable is that we should keep on pitching seed because there is good soil out there somewhere.

"I think it's too easy," I said about this takeaway the second time I heard it in as many weeks. I have a low tolerance for formal events, so I was already on edge (don't worry—the Lord's helping me with that). I'd read this parable dozens of times, but it struck me differently this time. Christians tend to use this parable as a copout for why people aren't coming to faith: too hard, rocky, or weed-riddled to produce anything good. *Why did God put us in this plot of land? God, if you had just given me better soil. The person seeing a harvest must have been given the good soil. Dumb soil.*

But hearing this parable read aloud, I couldn't make sense of it. Why didn't the farmer do a better job of marking the boundaries, tilling up the hardened ground, removing the rocks, and treating for weeds? Why was the farmer willing to leave so much to chance? If we are going to use a gardening metaphor, we need to remember that gardening is hard work—and that is the point. Evangelism doesn't begin at the point of searching for the best soil. It's about looking at a place where there is no garden and envisioning what could be there. It's about doing the hard work of sinking our shovels, our tillers, and our hands into the dirt and cultivating the ground. It is slow, hard, deliberate, patient work. It requires us to realize there are a lot of rocks out there, some of which are only revealed after difficult times, and when they emerge, we have to chuck them. Sometimes it will feel like we are making way, sinking our shovels deep into the soil, only to strike a hidden boulder. Tending the garden—what we will call *faithful presence*—means keeping an eye out for the budding weeds and removing them by the root when we see them. It means conditioning the soil with compassion, empathy, and love. It means building a retaining wall to ensure our harvest won't be lost when the storms of life come. It means consistent and intentional effort to bring forth and grow what wasn't there initially.

As Christians, I think we waste too much seed because we haven't done our part to tend the plot of land we've been given. We all want a good harvest, but we don't want to work the garden.

We all want a good harvest, but we want to reap it from the confines of our worship services and our buildings. That's like trying to harvest from the produce section at your local grocery store. Harvesting happens in the field—which is outside! Harvesting is work. Let's not blame the soil that wasn't adequately prepared to receive the seed. Let's show up, turn some soil, and condition it with godly nutrients. Then, when the time is right, plant and water the seeds.

Remember, you might be the one who tills but doesn't plant. Or you might inherit someone's tilled soil, ready for tending and planting. Or you may have the privilege of harvesting the work of another. Regardless, any good yield is because someone took on the hard work of caring for the soil. In this section, we are going to examine the work of cultivating good soil for receipt of the good news. Good newsing—lifestyle evangelism—is about sinking your hands into the soil of someone's life, planting seeds in a way that is conducive to that particular soil, and consistently watering and watching it mature.

four
NOT ALL *SOIL* IS THE *SAME*

To the Jews I became like a Jew, to win the Jews. To those under the law I became like one under the law (though I myself am not under the law), so as to win those under the law. To those not having the law I became like one not having the law (though I am not free from God's law but am under Christ's law), so as to win those not having the law. To the weak I became weak, to win the weak. I have become all things to all people so that by all possible means I might save some.

—1 Corinthians 9:20–22

Our neighbors and coworkers have names, and we need to know them. They have stories, and we need to listen. We have a God who loves us, and they have the same God who loves them.[1]

━━━━●━━━━━━●━━━━

1. Shauna Pilgreen, *Love Where You Live: How to Live Sent in the Place You Call Home* (Grand Rapids: Revell Publishing, 2019), 95.

Making Sense

So far we've talked about *soteriology*—the question of salvation. And we've talked about *eschatology*—the question of final things and God's preferred picture of all things. Now it's time for *hermeneutics*. Very simply put, hermeneutics is the art of making sense of things. Most often, hermeneutics is applied to text and literature. It is what happens when a reader looks at a text and gleans meaning from it.

How do we determine what the author intended? How does the text conform (or not) to its literary genre? What literary or rhetorical devices have been employed? What can we learn from the sentence structure and writing style? Is our perceived interpretation of the text the same thing as what the author intended to communicate? Can there be multiple meanings that are correct? Can a meaning be correct even if the author did not intend that meaning?

Have you ever taken a poetry class and realized how many students read the same poem differently? Have you ever noticed how Christians can look at the same passage of Scripture and derive two different meanings? That's hermeneutics—the art of making sense. But hermeneutics doesn't stop there. Have you ever received a text from a friend or a family member and been forced to "decode" it? What are they saying? Why is it in all caps? What does 'K' mean, and why didn't they say "okay"— are they mad? That's hermeneutics! We are always attempting to make sense of the world around us. Have you ever moved or visited somewhere and experienced culture shock because you realize they don't see the world the same way you've grown accustomed to seeing it? You have to work to understand what life and relationships in that new place mean. That's hermeneutics. We are always trying to make sense of things.

There is much that complicates the work of hermeneutics. Past experiences, implicit biases, cultural distance, pride, uninformed assumptions, naïveté, attribution errors, and a lack of curiosity can all contribute to diminished understanding. It's hard to make our way toward meaningful communication and connection without adequate understanding. In terms of relationships and evangelism, in terms of being a good newser, hermeneutics—making sense of one another—is part of the hard work of tending the soil. Without empathetic listening and learning, there is no effective evangelism and discipleship.

Hermeneutical Nomad

"But we are all Christians—how hard can it be?" Or, "We all live in the same country—how hard could it be?"

Far too many pastors have moved across the country to do ministry in a new place with these misinformed assumptions guiding their efforts. Certainly, experiencing a new culture does not mean someone will fail, but pastors and ministry leaders must use caution when entering a new context because what mattered and worked in one place might be received differently in another setting. We are presumptuous if we draw unwarranted conclusions about how we will be received—or, worse, do not even consider how we will be received—without doing the hard work of learning what life means in a specific time and place.

I'm a bit of a hermeneutical nomad. My life has felt like a constant process of attempting to find meaning in new places, among new people. I grew up in a small, rural-ish community in Ohio, just ten miles down I-77 from the steel town of Canton. I grew up in a very blue-collar atmosphere in the Midwest. I moved to Columbus, Ohio, for college, where I played football and was introduced to teammates from a variety of different backgrounds and learned that not all of them saw the world the way I saw it. I then enlisted in the military, shipped off to basic training, and was introduced to men and women of a variety of cultural backgrounds from all over the United States. We learned quickly that if anything meaningful were to happen there, we'd have to get really good at making sense of one another. I've lived in Monterey, California; in West Texas; in a military town in the American South (which is not the same as a regular town in the South); in a small, rural southern community; in a working-class community on the banks of a river in central Illinois (river culture is unique in its own way!). I now live in the heart of Chicago, just north of the famous Loop.

My life has been a constant process of bumping up against the lives of people who don't see, understand, or embrace the world the same way I do. As a pastor and a Christian, it has meant that each shift has forced me to enter spaces as a learner, without presumption, recognizing that connections are built on the backside of curiosity. Empathy is a prerequisite of evangelism. I've visited multiple countries outside the U.S., including Germany, Kosovo, Macedonia, Kenya, Costa Rica, and Panama. Wherever I've gone, I've recognized that to value people deeply, to see them the way the Lord sees them, to value their place in the kingdom of God, I must be willing to do the hard work of getting to know them, of attempting to make sense of them, to listen and learn from them. When we make the assumption that our canned presentation of the gospel will mean the same thing regardless of the context, we do more harm than good. Faithful good newsing starts with the commitment to recognize the interpretive distance between ourselves and others and commit to the kind of time, patience, presence, and empathy that are necessary for making sense of one another.

The Echo Chamber Effect

You might be thinking, *Jeff, that's great and all, but I've never traveled much, and I'm not a pastor who has moved across the country. I've lived in the same place all my life!* To that person I would say this: presumption is indiscriminate. For many of us, though we might be native to the places we live, it doesn't mean we are in a better position to make sense of those we find around us. Even in familiar contexts where we feel comfortable, there are a number of deficiencies that can contribute to our lack of understanding.

For example, we are all guilty of the echo chamber effect. We are more inclined to gravitate toward spaces where people already believe like we do, see the world as we see it, and constantly confirm our worldview. The choices we make about which news sources we trust, the sermons we listen to, the places we hang out—all of them work to solidify our perspectives and affirm our beliefs about the world and our place in it. The longer we hang out in our echo chambers, the more entrenched our assumptions become. Our way of seeing the world becomes the *only* reasonable way to see the world. The echo chamber teaches us that anyone whose view and vision for life is different from ours is a problem to fix instead of a person to connect and engage with. We enter into spaces to *convince* rather than *communicate*. Echo chambers mean we are inclined to understand the world through the perspectives and voices that most resemble our own.

Good newsing invites us beyond the boundaries of our echo chambers. Good newsing dispatches us into places of discomfort, among people who are unlike us. If we enter those spaces with the presumption of our own rightness and righteousness, we will miss opportunities to connect deeply, walk faithfully with others, and discern the unique and distinct connections of God's story with their stories. Even if we live in the same place our whole lives, we all must navigate and negotiate spaces of difference, learning how to make meaning of those we are most inclined to avoid. Christians who are committed to good newsing will remember that we are all, always, social novices who must take the time and make the commitment to understand who people are.

Go Outside and Play

Growing up, I navigated adolescence in a world where parents had yet to be called helicopters. They were less protective (though not negligent) and more trusting of their own neighborhoods and communities. In the summer, when the sun beat hot and kids were tempted to settle in and watch TV or play video games, the constant refrain from our parents was, "Go outside and play!" Don't stay inside. The world of exploration, awe, fun, and fascination is outside—go there! (As long as you are back by dinner.)

When I arrived in the church, I felt like the common mantra among churches was the opposite of what parents told kids when I was growing up. Instead of *Go out there and play*, it became, *Come in here and stay*. I don't know that this was intentional, but it was definitely reinforced in the culture. When you become a Christian, you are extracted from your environment and placed in a context that is filled with classes, events, and expectations that further distance you from your point of origin—the "worldly" place you came from. The longer you are in church, the more disconnected from the context of the worldly community you become. If you grew up in church, it's entirely possible to spend so much time in the echo chamber of Christianity, the church, and the Christian subculture, that you might know nothing or very little of the people outside the tightly enclosed group to which you belong. That is the danger of *come in here and stay*.

Let me extend a bit of grace here. I understand the temptation even though I don't agree with the practice. The world outside can feel dangerous, confusing, threatening. We want to preserve and protect our holiness against the onslaught of temptations that are eager to wrap their thorny branches around our lives. The church community is a safe place. Especially in larger congregations, the church building can become a smorgasbord of activities with events for the whole family: movie nights, date nights, seminars and trainings, youth events, play groups for younger children, financial classes, and more. Some megachurches have their own bookstores, barbershops, and even workout spaces.

You can legitimately spend most of your non-work time among those who belong to the same group and visit the same facility as you do several times a week. There was a season of my ministry when I spent so much time moving from event to event within the church building each week that I suddenly realized I had very few non-church friends or connections.

We need leaders and churches who are committed to going and playing outside the church. The work of good newsing is outside! As a missional theologian, I'm absolutely committed to the belief that our God is a sending God. God dispatches us into the discomfort of settings that are often at odds with our commitments and convictions. God sends us outside to play, into the wide-open places where people are, where we explore and rediscover awe, where we have fun and are fascinated. We become strategic in the places we go, the people we meet, the conversations we have, and the relationships we forge.

Katie Rawson notes, "We are sent into the world by Jesus just as he was sent by the Father. With the Spirit of the Father and Jesus inside us, we display Jesus to the world, just as he embodied and displayed the Father. As Jesus entered our world and drew us into his world—the community of Father, Son, and Spirit—we are to enter the worlds of others and draw them into the community of Jesus."[2] Outside the boundaries of our echo chambers and the confines of our churches, we discover fields rich with potential harvest, lives to be connected to the hope of Jesus, and those to be recruited into God's kingdom purposes.

---

2. Katie J. Rawson, *Crossing Cultures with Jesus: Sharing Good News with Sensitivity and Grace* (Downers Grove, IL: InterVarsity Press, 2015), 13.

You Are a Missionary

Are you starting to feel like a missionary yet? Good! That's the goal. Too often we've been tempted to believe that both evangelism and missionary work are the call of a select few Christians. Though there are specific ways that those responsibilities and callings might be worked out formally, the work of missionary evangelism—or what we've been calling good newsing—is the work of all followers of Jesus.

Luke is a master storyteller. Of all the Gospel writers, I'm drawn to Luke the most. Sometimes we want to read the Gospels as a series of short stories, missing the narrative coherence that connects everything together. Luke is doing something intentional in his Gospel. Luke starts his telling about the ministry of Jesus with the kingdom declaration from Isaiah 61: good news for the poor, recovery of sight for the blind, freedom for slaves, and release for captives. It's good news. Then Luke shares the stories that demonstrate the efficacy of that declaration. Jesus does what he says, and he recruits others to join him. Are you making the connections? Remember when I said that God has wired this world to co-labor with humanity? It's this. Jesus calls others to apprentice him in this kingdom way. They walk with him and learn from him, and then Jesus deploys them—first he sends 12 in Luke 9, then 72 in Luke 10, then 120 in Acts 2 (which is considered volume 2 of Luke's storytelling.)

Jesus announces, demonstrates, recruits, instructs, and dispatches. Followers of Jesus are immediately given the purpose of going out into the world as those who are representative of God's good-newsing mission. They are missionaries in the sense that, wherever they are, wherever they go, they are called to represent the good-news mission. Good newsing operates under this same assumption. We can't hang out forever in the produce section with the freshly picked harvest. We have to go into the fields, into the plots of land that need tilled, cultivated, conditioned, and seeded. We are a sent people.

Of course, it will not be easy work. It might mean we have to schedule less and do less at the physical structure of the church building so we have more time to do what should be done away from the building. We mustn't miss our post-COVID opportunity. The pandemic had a significant impact on the church—both positive and negative. One of the positives is that it has broken the dependence of people on the physical activities and programs of the church. They've been away, and we are learning that many aren't eager to come back as often as they once did. We must leverage this disruption to train, equip, and empower believers to spend more time where they work, live, and play as lifestyle evangelists, bearing witness to the good news of Jesus.

Missionary work is uncomfortable and awkward. We have to go into spaces we are accustomed to avoiding, among people of whom we are often suspicious—and they of us!—with a learner's spirit that seeks to understand instead of seeking to fix. Authentic, good-newsing missionary work can lead to deep connections and disheartening rejections. But the call is clear: *Go out and play!*

Knowing Place

One of the most unfortunate implications of the church's missionary work throughout history is that much of that work has been devoid of context. It's been both imperialistic in its attitude and colonizing in its efforts. Christians show up—often from the West to places that are very unlike the West—and determine the deficiency of the setting where they arrive. They then seek to impose not only a belief system but also a cultural way of life on people for whom there is little to no connection. Under pressure, some might capitulate to the missionary, but the practice of Christianity bears little resemblance to the unique context of the people. This forced disconnect has led to a loss of cultural heritage, the hegemony of cultural assumptions from the West, and a homogeneity that strips the mosaic of God's beautiful diversity of its differences. This kind of mission work doesn't attend to place because it doesn't believe that place matters. It operates under the assumption that people are generally the same no matter where we go.

Good newsers don't embrace those assumptions. They realize that place does matter. There are certain types of plants and produce that grow well in certain types of soil. It's important to know the soil and understand the plot of ground where one is planting. I'm always amazed at how often the Bible notes the names of the places where Jesus visits. If you track the stories of the Gospels, you will recognize that the community matters. It has implications and can even determine the reception of Jesus by people in that community.

When I was called to Chicago, I recognized immediately the deficiency of my knowledge. Chicago is huge—2.7 million people! Six years prior, I had lived in a town of 2,000 in a county of 8,000. So Chicago's size felt a little overwhelming, to say the least. I knew I needed to get to know the city, so I started reading any book I could find on Chicago. What I quickly came to discover is that, as much as we outsiders speak about Chicago as a whole, actual Chicagoans tend to speak about the city by its neighborhood areas. Learning about the context became increasingly complicated. One could learn about the history of the Northside, Westside, and Southside. But within those areas, one had to be careful not to draw conclusions about a whole section based on the history or present activities in one or two neighborhood areas. Though the Southside is predominantly Black, the Westside is predominantly Black and Latinx, and the Northside is predominantly white, there were internal distinctions to be made in those areas based on affluence, education, investment, and ethnicity. There is a complicated history in Chicago. Likewise, Chicago has a unique spiritual history and setting. Deeply impacted by Catholicism, it's moving toward post-Christendom but has yet to arrive fully. Megachurches still play a major role in the Southside Black community, and church-planting efforts are still active throughout the city. Knowing the context means knowing the politics, the narrative assumptions, and the realities of ethnic segregation. Although Chicago is one of the most diverse cities in the United States, its complicated history has left it the most racially segregated city, which has significant implications for collaboration, networking, trust, and bearing witness to the good news of Jesus.

My friend Jon said once, "I've lived here ten years, and I con-sistently feel like a novice in the city." The work of the gospel will be dependent on knowledge of the city.

This wasn't my first rodeo. I've always been fascinated by place. When I move into a town, I want to know what makes this place tick. What are the significant and systemic needs of the com-munity? Where does joy break in? What breaks the hearts of the people? What are the stories people tell about the commu-nity that offer glimpses into what they believe about their lives and their place in this world? When I moved to the small, rural community of Erin, Tennessee, I spent the first several months traveling throughout the community every Thursday, visiting with many of the senior citizens—who, in a community like that, are the curators of cultural knowledge. When I moved to Pekin, Illinois, I had a meeting scheduled with the mayor within the first couple of weeks. I asked hard questions and found out I had just moved to what she called "the meth capital of Illinois." That was a sobering discovery that would impact the trajectory of our ministry in that place.

Bearing witness to the gospel is *contextual*. What does it look like there? Being a good newser means getting to know the place that continues to shape the lives and imaginations of the people who live there. The authors of *The New Parish* suggest, "Without a recovery of place, the missional movement can end up being driven by the issue of the day. It is the mundane particularity of your place that grounds the missional impulse in the real world. Only as we seek to follow Jesus into the distinc-tiveness of our respective places are we invited to demonstrate our love of God by loving our neighbors."[3] Without this curiosity, we are often tossing the wrong seed into the wrong soil. We will fail to make sense *to* the context because we've not done the hard work of making sense *of* that context.

How much do you know about a place? Yes, you've lived there, but I've been amazed when I've asked how little longtime residents of a place can tell me about their community. What is the spiritual atmosphere? What history might impact one's reception of the good news? What's the political environment, and how does that impact people? What are the social issues, the systemic injustices, the felt needs of the community? What are the cultural elements that shape people's interactions and relationships with one another? These questions matter. Getting to know the place matters. Good newsing takes context seriously and seeks to plant the good news in soil that makes sense.

Knowing People

The work of contextual knowledge for the sake of faithful good newsing is not an abstract concept. As much as you can learn from books, knowing a place is about knowing people. People must become the obsession of good newsers. Okay, introverts, hold on for a moment! There are some who are far more comfortable than others with getting out and about and meeting folks. For instance, I can talk to anyone, anywhere. I can initiate conversations. I love people. Other people are shy, or

---

3. Paul Sparks, Tim Soerens, and Dwight J. Friesen, *The New Parish: How Neighborhood Churches Are Transforming Mission, Discipleship, and Community* (Downers Grove, IL: InterVarsity Press, 2014), 45.

uncomfortable in unfamiliar settings, and might not be excited about initiating. I'm not suggesting that everyone do this the same way. Leverage your own personality. Jesus sends people out in twos. I've always wondered if that's because combined strengths make for more meaningful connections. Extroverts are great on the front end. Introverts can be better at going deep once we get past initial engagement. But the call remains: become people-obsessed.

Understanding comes from proximity and connection. Jesus was people-obsessed. He sought to know people, to be with them, to hear their stories, to learn of their concerns and fears. He didn't treat everyone the same—he embraced them in their uniqueness. Jesus made the Samaritan woman at the well in John 4 a priority in a different way than the way he made the tax collector Zacchaeus in Luke 19 a priority. Each person had a unique story that Jesus sought to understand so that the good news he proclaimed would make sense to the person with whom he shared proximity and connection.

Becoming people-obsessed is different from meeting people in passing. Making connections is different than extending the scope of your acquaintances. Knowing people means showing up and asking meaningful questions. It means peering into the deeper, below-the-surface realities of their lives, their world-views, values, fears, and aspirations. It means learning how poverty or wealth, a traditional nuclear family or an alternative family structure shaped their lives. It means understanding how their ethnicity or racial heritage has shaped their perception of relationships, safety, and trust. It means understanding the cultural peculiarities that might be potential points of disconnection or landmines for someone "not from around here." It means being able to meet people without initial offense or judgment. It means becoming insatiably curious.

The work of good newsing requires a commitment to the art of making sense. We seek to know—not to manipulate others but as a recognition of the inherent worth and dignity we afford all who bear the image of God. We seek to know—recognizing that the location of a person's life may shape their sensitivity toward the good news we represent. We seek to know—because being known is more important than telling people *what* we know.

five
MY
COFFEE SHOP

Paul entered the synagogue and spoke boldly there for
three months, arguing persuasively about the kingdom of
God. But some of them became obstinate; they refused to
believe and publicly maligned the Way. So Paul left them.
He took the disciples with him and had discussions daily in
the lecture hall of Tyrannus. This went on for two years, so
that all the Jews and Greeks who lived in the province of
Asia heard the word of the Lord.

—Acts 19:8–10

But once the followers of Christ in a neighborhood begin to envision themselves as the local church instead of the building—
once they see the parish as the place where they live out their
faith—every building becomes a potential church building. They
all become sacred space for worship, mission, formation, and
community. Each one is one marked by our concern for their
ongoing renewal and redemptive purposing.[1]

●————————————●

1. Sparks, Soerens, and Friesen, *The New Parish*, 147.

I Love Christians—Just Not That Much

I get spiritually claustrophobic quickly. I came to faith in the military at the age of twenty-five. After years of incredibly dysfunctional behavior with an equally dysfunctional marriage of three years, the Lord seized on a moment of immense vulnerability. I was deployed to the Balkans, separated from my two toddler sons, prepping for an impending divorce on my return home, and I found myself sitting in a little army chapel at midnight in Skopje, Macedonia. There in that chapel, I heard what I could only later attribute to the voice of the Lord offering me an ultimatum: *Jeff, if you come to me, I will save you, your family, and your marriage—but you will give me the rest of your life. If not, it all falls apart from here.* This was the moment. As awkwardly and in whatever clunky way I could, I found myself confessing my brokenness and yielding my life to Jesus. To say this led to a radical change would be a grand understatement. I was a ringleader of debauchery in my platoon, and now I felt deeply compelled to study and read the Bible as often as I could and go to every church service I could find. It didn't matter if it was Protestant or Catholic—if it had something to do with Jesus, I was there. I would go to a charismatic Black service on Sundays on my post and attend RCA (Catholic adult confirmation classes) on Tuesdays. I couldn't get enough.

But not only had everything changed, I was also immediately in the fray. I was not whisked away into the security of holy huddles. I was with my soldiers, and they were trying to figure out what had happened to their sergeant. They were watching, testing, and at times teasing my newfound faith. They were waiting for me to stumble, trip up, betray my quest for Jesus.

And I loved every minute of it. It didn't take much Bible reading to realize that perhaps this was part of the package. If we are to be lights in the world, of course there are going to be moments when people try to snuff out our wicks. I felt immensely privileged to spend each and every day living out my faith among my fellow soldiers and colleagues. I worked hard not to play the holier-than-thou card. I couldn't stand those kind of people when I was a raging heathen. I didn't ask anyone to adjust their behavior, their language, or their actions for me. I was not about to impose my faith on others. Instead, when I discovered that Jesus had commissioned the church to live as witnesses, I simply saw myself as a representative. From August 2001 (my yes-to-Jesus moment) to February 2003 (my departure from military life), I lived with and among my friends and comrades. My life constantly bumped up against others who did not share my faith, and I loved it. I had the privilege of baptizing one of my soldiers just prior to his deployment.

Then, after I left the military and began dipping my toes into my calling, I landed my first part-time pastorate at the church I attended. I was excited. I now had the freedom to devote most of my time and energy to the work of the church, to discipling the people of God, and to growing the church. Sitting in an office, surrounded by my books, and obligated to various meetings and teams and committees, I thought, *This is the life*—until I realized it wasn't. As good as the work was that we did, I felt like I was suffocating. I found that I can only be in predominantly Christian settings for so long before I go stir-crazy. Not that I don't love the church! I think I just love being around nonbelievers more.

Shoney's kept me sane on the front end after my transition from the army. The church I worked for could only pay me a nominal salary—hardly enough to support a family—so I worked twenty to thirty hours a week as a host, cashier, and busboy at Shoney's. Yes, I was a twenty-seven-year-old, college-degree-holding, former military linguist with top-secret security clearance filling up the egg buffet and carrying off food scraps. But most mornings I was with people who weren't Jesus followers. Some were hardened antagonists toward the church, like my boss (he eventually softened). He'd give me such a hard time about my faith. Others were merely skeptical. Some were curious. I had the best conversations between rushes. I had the privilege of baptizing one of my coworkers shortly after I left that job, and two of my coworkers attended our church on Sunday mornings when they didn't work (which wasn't many— which is why we need alternative worship opportunities for service-industry people, but that's a topic for a different book).

After moving into full-time church work, my claustrophobia grew. I had to search for opportunities to be outside the church. I served as our church's campus minister at the local state university. I coached my son's sports teams, kept a secondary office at the local Starbucks, and tried to join about every community committee I could. I needed to be with non-believing people—those for whom the Jesus story had little meaning, who'd been jaded by their interaction with Christians and the church, and those disconnected from the hope I believed so deeply in. I committed to show up in their space. I was at Starbucks so often I had an unofficial designated table in the afternoons and late evenings. I became a pseudo-counselor to the baristas as many came to chat with me on their breaks about their lives, their hurts, and their celebrations. I had the privilege of baptizing one of my baristas and officiating his wedding. He eventually played for the worship band in the church I planted.

I love Christians—just not that much! I love the fellowship of believers. I've been immensely thankful for all the ways fellow followers of Jesus have made space for my family and me. I am committed to growing with and loving deeply those who call themselves Christian. However, this love is shaped by what Alan Hirsch in his book *Forgotten Ways* calls *"communitas"*— fellowship on mission.[2] My love for the church is shaped by a love for the common mission of the church. I love the church because together—despite our peculiarities, quirks, neuroses, and inconsistencies—we've been bound together in this beau- tifully redemptive kingdom mission. We've been woven together as a tapestry to demonstrate to the world the glory of God. If it were not for that collective mission, I'm not convinced I'd be around as often. I would probably opt for other Sunday morning activities. I have often told my congregations, "If it weren't for the cross, resurrection, and commissioning of Jesus, I'd be golf- ing on Sunday mornings." There's nothing all that compelling to me about just showing up once a week to "do church." I want to live on mission. Living on mission—living as a good news- er—demands a consistent, intentional commitment to show up where the church *isn't*, but *should* be. Sometimes those spaces are obvious. Other times they demand creativity.

---

2. Alan Hirsch, *The Forgotten Ways: Reactivating Apostolic Movements* (Grand Rapids: Brazos Press, 2016), 162.

What if Jesus Meant It?

"As you are going, make disciples." This is (part of) the Great Commission of Jesus. It often reads, "Go" in English. However, the reading of this text in Greek gives the sense that the imperative is rooted in the assumption that we are *already* going. This subtle shift in nuance can have profound impact on how we view and carry out our mission as Christ followers. We become so accustomed to our echo-chambered lives that we have to be compelled to "go" out where we've not been going. Somewhere along the way, we stopped going—and that is unfortunate. We need to be *told* to go. This failure to go is represented in the fact that I teach a master's level course on "Christian neighboring." We literally need to be taught how to neighbor when Jesus specifically tied that concept to faithful love. So I love the "as you are going" variation on the Great Commission. As you are going about life—wherever you live, work, and play—make disciples. Be going about your business, showing up in the lives of others, and demonstrating the good news. This would be a good thing.

What if Jesus meant that? What if core to the life of the church is the as-you-are-going life—one that deliberately shows up and demonstrates the evidence of the good news and an invitation to come and see, get a little closer, and discover what apprenticing Jesus is all about? When we take "as you are going" seriously, something shifts in the church. We become less obsessed by the internalized trivialities that seem to dot the landscape of church conflict, and we become more mission-focused instead, being consistently reminded of the immense privilege and responsibility of connecting with those who are disconnected from Jesus.

We have to show up. We have to be creative. We have to be strategic. We have to be compelling.

Going Native

Upon departing a community of 130,000 people in a military town that I was accustomed to and comfortable in—one that my wife and I still consider home—I moved to a small community of 2,000 people in a county of 8,000 people in the heart of rural Tennessee. This had *never* been my context. There was no Starbucks in town! In fact, we were forty-five minutes from the nearest Starbucks. Life in this town was very different from what I had experienced in the previous nearly two decades of my life. The church was amazing! The people were great! But like I said, I get twitchy when I have to hang out in the office throughout the week. I knew that if I were going to be faithful to my calling, I had to show up! I had to find places *to* show up. I had to go full-on native.

If you are not "from there"—do you love the people enough to go native? Do you love them enough to immerse yourself in the contextual life? Do you love them enough to learn their rhythms and patterns, figure out their hangouts, and develop an interest in their passions? Good newsers learn to put on the skin of their community and fall in love.

There was no Starbucks, but there was a Fitz's Restaurant and BJ's Diner. Each morning the gatekeepers of the community—the stewards of the political power and historical knowledge—

gathered for coffee and breakfast at one of these two places. I made a commitment of showing up for breakfast in these places a couple of times a week. I wanted to make myself familiar to them. I took up hunting. I'd never hunted a day in my life, and up to that point I didn't even own a gun. However, I knew that if I were going to get close to the men of the community, I would have to don the camo and lie on the wet ground early in the morning.

I ended up coaching high school and middle school football. In small, rural Southern towns, Friday night football in the fall makes the world go 'round. Because of my experience playing college ball and their recent string of abysmal seasons, they asked if I could help out, so from July through November, I volunteered with the local teams from 2:30 p.m. to 7:30 p.m.—and the church endorsed it. They knew that if they asked me to hang out in my office all the time, I might lose my mind.

For four seasons I coached and connected with coaches and players who had little understanding of the hope of Jesus. Some of my team started attending church, and I had the privilege of baptizing some. (Side note: Coaching football in a small town gains you great credibility, especially among the gatekeepers in the community—until you lose. The same guys who excitedly talked to me on Friday mornings at Fitz's had nothing to say to me on Monday mornings after a loss.)

Being a good newser in a new context required me to go native. Much of the bad news of Christianity is rooted in a history of expecting people to meet us where *we* are and failing to meet them where *they* are (and *how* they are).

My Coffee Shop

For many, when the COVID crisis struck, the feeling of church "shutting down" caused an angst like the church in the West has rarely experienced. It was hard. My own angst began on March 16, 2020, two days after my last visit to *my* coffee shop. That was the day the coffee shop shut down. Almost a year earlier, my wife and I had made a significant leap. After pastoring part- or full-time for more than fifteen years, I had accepted an associate professor role at a university, as well as a calling to the city of Chicago to serve as an urban missionary leading Reach77, a church-type mission seeking strategic incarnational presence in the city and working with Chicago-area church plants and planters. Six years earlier, we had lived in a town of 2,000. We now lived in a city of 2.7 million—yeah, not the same thing. To make matters more interesting, the last two moves we'd made, we had made as pastors to communities with churches that were waiting on us. We had an in-built network of relationships and then had to figure out the community. We arrived in Chicago on May 21, 2019—and no one cared. We knew few and had no one waiting our arrival.

We landed, unpacked, and ate some pizza. I asked myself, *Where do we start?* Then I thought, *If I were in a small community, where would I go to meet people? I'd go to the diner, the coffee shop, the sports field—whatever it took.* So the very next morning, I got up early and walked two blocks from my house to the coffee shop on the main road that connected our neighborhood with public transportation. I sat. I read. I watched. The following morning, I did the same. And the next after that. I woke up early and started showing up, buying a coffee each morning. Show up consistently enough, and you start to notice the regulars. That's how I met Alyssa and Ryan, whom I described in the introduction. I'm also not a shy person, so I have no problem striking up conversations and butting in. People say, read, and do fascinating things! I will step in, ask questions, and admire them.

I met my friend Shadi, a Lebanese Muslim, because he and his wife-to-be were sitting next to me talking about their wedding plans. I mentioned to them that I had officiated more than fifty weddings and that I was thoroughly excited for them. We became friends. I met my friend Lauren—an artist, activist, and community organizer—because she was reading a fascinating book that I wanted to know more about. That question led to a friendship where we consistently get together for coffee and "try to figure out how to save the world," as our spouses call it. I met my friend Ben, the "following Jesus without drama or dogma" guy, at the coffee shop. He's a successful entrepreneur with a wonderful heart and a passion for the city. I met Brett and Amanda, a professor and a doctor, respectively. They are two of the best people I know, and their son now calls us Aunt Angie and Uncle Jeff. I know all the baristas. They introduce me to other people, and friendships are forged. I've become affectionately known by the baristas as "the mayor of Armitage"—a title that humbles me and reminds me of my responsibility to steward that space well.

When my coffee shop shut down, it felt like my church had closed. This was my space of building relationships and strategic connections. Moving forward, I had to be even more intentional. I went on socially distanced walks with my neighbors and friends from the coffee shop. Early on in COVID, my son and I made donut runs and drop-offs to our new friends. We Zoomed for birthday parties. We sat outside. We stayed connected. When the shop reopened and I was able to return to "my" table, more than one barista said that seeing me sit there made it feel like normalcy had returned.

I love Adam, Jason, Kate, Tup, Jonathan, and all the others I've had the privilege of getting to know. Most are not religious or interested in Christianity. However, when I stop by on my way to church to preach, they are the first to cheer me on. We care about one another. We are friends.

The Four Ps

So where do we start? That's a great question. As I've examined my life throughout the years and attempted to understand what has transpired as I've intentionally entered into space with those who do not share my worldview, a few elements continue to bubble to the surface. Proximity, presence, presumption, and peace-making are necessary postures for "as you are going" living.

Proximity

We get nowhere if we don't go somewhere. The first step is the commitment to show up. As good newsers, we have to make a commitment to show up and share proximity with people who are not in our church, part of our family, in our echo chamber, or connected to our faith. I've been astounded throughout the years how few Christians can point to the meaningful relationships they have with people who are not in their churches. Few Christians can even tell you the names or anything meaningful about their neighbors! We've got to go out and play. As a former pastor, I give you permission to say no to a few church events and yes to more opportunities to show up where the church isn't.

Where do people hang out? Where is the pulse of the community? Where do people gather to establish meaningful relationships? Is there a running club, a duck blind, or a diner you can start showing up regularly to? Is there a community organization—Kiwanis, Rotary, Chamber of Commerce—that you can join? Are Friday nights under the lights in the fall a big deal, or high school basketball? Go. Get out and go! Just know that when you do go, when you show up, people will be watching. Don't go to a high school basketball game and then lose your mind and act a fool. Go and demonstrate a loving, kind, compelling posture.

Presence

Showing up is the start, but it's not sufficient. It's not enough to ask, "Where am I going?" I must also ask, "To whom am I going?" We show up not simply to be there but also to be *with*. Proximity must lead to presence. I've met many Christians who go but never connect, which is unfortunate. The going we do as Christians is an exercise in vulnerability and connection. We prayerfully go, asking God to open opportunities for us to connect deeply with others. Proximity says, "I'm here." Presence says, "I'm here *for you*." We learn to take small, what can feel like risky, steps to engage, to meet, to ask questions, to get to know names. Please get to know names! Nothing communicates value like ensuring you know the names of the people with whom you connect.

Presence means taking a keen interest in others. Presence means living at an unhurried pace with an undistracted attention. If we are there but not there because we are eagerly trying to get somewhere else or are absorbed in our social media, we are not present. We learn to sit with, share with, laugh with, learn from, and care deeply for real people with real stories in those spaces. It's not enough for me to know that Tup is my barista. I also need to know that Tup is an aspiring musical studio producer who works late into the night with artists in his production startup and opens the coffee shop early in the morning. I need to know he will finally be able to fully pursue his dreams of full-time production when he can make three times his rent monthly before stepping out. I need to know about Tup!

Presumption

Christians are often conditioned for presumption. Entering into space as a good newser means recognizing the tendency to show up with an agenda, with a set of prescribed answers, and with certain judgments about the space we've entered. This is not uncommon, but it can lead to unfortunate implications. To show up well doesn't mean we necessarily abandon all our commitments and convictions. That would be disingenuous, and I've yet to meet someone who doesn't embrace Christianity expect us to do that. But it means we hold our commitments and convictions in open palms instead of white-knuckled fists. It means we become increasingly aware of the filters we wear in seeing others and making sense of them. Being a faithful good newser means we can suspend our judgments.

One of the most difficult issues for many Christians in post-Christianizing and secularizing culture is the fear of the culture wars and that the embrace of a person means the embrace of their lifestyle. With good intention, we say things like, "love the sinner, hate the sin." How about if we started instead with, "love your neighbor as yourself"? Love doesn't begin at the point of differentiating what there is to hate. Love begins at the point of seeing the image of God in each and every person we come across, just as we would long for them to do for us. I love others in the same way I want to be loved. I wouldn't want to be written off because of a perceived belief about who I am, positions I hold, or encounters the person has had with other people who are like me. I wouldn't want to be loved *despite* the choices I make. I would simply want to be loved. I should therefore want to extend that same love to others.

I want to be fascinated by people, insatiably curious. I want to hear their heart and share space with them without immediately assuming I'll have to just tolerate them. I ought to want to know the story or stories that inform their existence. This might give me greater insight as to why they live as they do and choose as they do. I love not as a veiled attempt to put up with those kinds of people but as a deep commitment to all people in the same way that Jesus is committed to me.

Peace-making

Finally—and this has been pivotal for my life as a good news-er—we must be persons of peace, peacemakers, as we are going. We are living in a world where people are consistently primed for a fight. They are used to bumping up against those whose differences immediately poise them for division. Every-one has something to defend, define, or debate. People become increasingly leery of broaching difficult subjects or making personal revelations because they never know, "Where's the trigger? What's the litmus test that will ultimately leave me cut out from their life?"

But Jesus says, "Blessed are the peace*makers*," not the peace-*finders*. Making peace is an active posture of love, em-pathy, compassion, and kindness. It means meeting insult with blessing and entering a charged environment with a non-anx-ious presence. It means that, instead of slapping back, we take the shot and offer grace. Christians sometimes let themselves be easily provoked because we've been taught to believe we are always under threat of losing our footing in this world and that we must stand our ground. What if, instead of a well-rehearsed response to a perceived slight, we instead say, "Tell me more about why you feel like that"? Disrupt the tension with a pos-ture of peace.

six

READING THE *ROOM*

When Jesus reached the spot, he looked up and said to him, "Zacchaeus, come down immediately. I must stay at your house today." So he came down at once and welcomed him gladly. All the people saw this and began to mutter, "He has gone to be the guest of a sinner." But Zacchaeus stood up and said to the Lord, "Look, Lord! Here and now I give half of my possessions to the poor, and if I have cheated anybody out of anything, I will pay back four times the amount."

—Luke 19:5–8

Sometimes we must open the space to invite people to ask their questions about Jesus. We cultivate their curiosity as we work on building our own. As you begin practicing living as a sent person, growing a curious heart will deeply bless those around you.[1]

1. Holleman and Holleman, *Sent*, 155.

Insatiable Curiosity

My friend Todd—church planter, college professor, and all around amazing human being—suggests that all discipleship (and, as a consequence, evangelism) begins at the point of insatiable curiosity about people. In some respects, this is a bit of a flip of the script. Too often, both discipleship and evangelism begin with what we have to say rather than who the person is. We operate under the assumption, *We have the truth. They need the truth. We tell them the truth. Life is better.* Unfortunately, failure to attend to the person devalues the dignity of that person, the uniqueness of what makes them who they are, and it can create a disconnect between who they are and what we suggest the truth means. Evangelism as good newsing doesn't begin with the assumption that we are homogenous human souls all in need of the master key that unlocks the door to paradise beyond. Instead, good newsing operates under the assumption that each human being has been uniquely stitched together by God, a mosaic of brilliant difference, forming a beauty that is bound up in convoluted stories, brokenness, and, yes, sin. This beauty—when met by the faithful witness of a good newser who takes a keen interest in each person—is unearthed through the dance of curiosity, compassion, kindness, care, and a capacity to point to the One who gives full flight to the beauty of their lives.

Insatiable curiosity is a skill to be learned. In a frenetic world where we move past one another, often tipping our hats as an extension of hurried cordiality, curiosity is hard to come by. It requires a pace that can afford people time to settle in, listen, and love well. It's the shift from proximity to presence. Insatiable curiosity is born of a heart of love, not dogmatic rigidity, self-righteousness, or moral superiority. The traditional religious mindset sits above others, looking down upon others, only interested in others enough to tell them what they should know. Not so with insatiable curiosity. Each person is a beautiful enigma, a divine mystery, a wonderfully complicated story longing to be known. Insatiable curiosity produces question askers, not answer givers.

Now, I *do* believe Jesus is the answer for the whole of human existence. I believe that with all my heart. I'm just not sure that Jesus was ever meant to be marketed like a cheap commodity, devoid of his desire for each unique person. When I witness Jesus with people in the Gospels, there are no canned approaches, only contextual connections born of intimacy and relationship. In John 4, he hangs out with the woman at the well and unearths deep-seated insecurities, theological peculiarities, and potential. For the chief tax collector Zacchaeus in Luke 19, Jesus calls him from his perch and stays with him overnight, sharing space and a meal and helping him discover how to leverage all he has to make an immense difference. The difference Jesus makes is rooted in the particularity of each person, their story, and what has shaped their way of being and seeing the world. Being people-obsessed and insatiably curious means that we find people to be fascinating. "Tell me more" is the constant refrain of the good newser. We demonstrate an inquisitiveness that often startles people who are more accustomed to the kinds of relationships where everyone is vying for a way to talk about themselves. Demonstrating interest is a reflection of care.

I love living in the city of Chicago because I'm on story overload constantly. Living in a city of 2.7 million people, a city filled with some of the most colorful characters, diverse people groups, and contrasting worldviews, I'm in good-newsing hog heaven. I love to people-watch in parks, on city streets, and in coffee shops. I'm fascinated by what makes people tick. I want to know, understand, and have my life impacted by their stories.

Beyond my coffee shop, my wife and I live on a busy corner on the edge of our neighborhood shopping district. We have no outdoor space of our own—no patio, balcony, deck, or anything. In the summer and fall we put our fold-out chairs on the corner and sit and read, drink coffee, and just hang out. We meet people. I love it. People stop by and chat. And that's when my curiosity kicks in. I want to know more about them. At one point during COVID, my wife and I had about eight people from all walks of life, socially distanced on our corner, sharing life together. My neighbor—a brilliant, successful consultant, devout, progressive Catholic, with a penchant for four-letter words, and with whom I have some of the most heated political debates— said, "You should just put up a sign here on the outside wall: 'Church meets here.'" And yes. It does. He used "church" to mean a space where diverse people could connect in wonderfully curious ways.

Curiosity breeds the authenticity of faith connections. The more we learn from, listen to, and love others, the more we recognize the beautiful, non-contrived connections between Jesus and their values, fears, and aspirations. The more we listen, the more often opportunities to make those connections will bubble to the surface naturally and organically, instead of being manipulated and imposed awkwardly on conversations with others based on an assumed agenda or unnecessary urgency.

A Soldier, a Police Officer, and a Drug Dealer

The title for this section sounds like a good set up for an *NCIS* episode or crime thriller. Sorry to disappoint. Each label the recognition that the good news we speak is born of a curiosity about those we find ourselves sharing life with. Each identity also highlights the importance of understanding that the truth of the good news must make sense within the context of each unique story.

A Soldier

When I first met my friend the soldier, it was one of the most painfully awkward spiritual first dates I've been on. He didn't want to be there, to say the least. We were sitting down to coffee together because his fiancée had requested it. They were suffering through an extremely dysfunctional season of their relationship. He was one of the hardest of the hard soldiers, special forces, deployed often, and wore the battle-tested, hardened bravado of someone who wasn't all that interested in sharing his feelings, especially with the likes of me. He was unimpressed with me, with my title, and with my eagerness to hear his story. He used language that I'm certain he hoped would offend me, the pastor. He was coarse, disinterested, and at times attempted to be intimidating. I have trained and been deployed with special-forces soldiers, and while I've always respected their professional competence, I'm unimpressed by machismo. Having grown up in a blue-collar world and spent time as an NCO in the military, I can snark back with the best of them. I'm also not easily intimidated. So we did a bit of an alpha-male dance, and we made it through our first meeting. My probing felt forced. But I'm stubborn and persistent, and his fiancée was desperate. So we met again and again.

I could speak his language, and as I got to know him, I learned that he cared deeply for his fiancée but was skeptical about Christianity. He was logical and science-minded. He'd met Christians who seemed critical of his job without understanding his sacrifices. He didn't have time or interest in "trafficking in fairytales and myths." His world was real, hard, and sometimes brutal. Between his deployments, a slow and steady friendship emerged between us. He witnessed the shifts taking place in his fiancée and her kids as they became increasingly interested in their faith. One of his coworkers started attending our church, and he saw the changes in him as well. He would have sniffed out a canned approach a mile away, so I didn't use one. I took my time. I shared my story of emerging from atheism when he asked. We wrestled with Jesus a bit.

The tipping point came at the point of his return from a particularly difficult deployment. He entered my office, shut the door, and displayed emotion for the first time. Everything had gone wrong during this latest deployment, and the lack of downtime had finally pushed him to the brink. In his world, there is no talking about one's struggles for fear of appearing weak. But he felt safe expressing himself to me. He wept, and I wept with him. We prayed together. After that, I witnessed the real journey of apprenticing Jesus begin. His breakthrough led to an interest in church, in reading the Bible, and a curiosity about

Jesus and faith. Eventually I performed his wedding. No canned or formulaic maneuvers would have worked with him. Only steady attention to his rational mind, his no-nonsense world-view, and his bottled-up pain could make the story of Jesus comprehensible to him. He wasn't looking for an eternal escape hatch. He was looking for a way of making meaning of his life on earth.

A Police Officer

"I regularly see the worst of the worst of humanity, and it honestly makes me doubt the goodness of God."

These were the words my police officer friend spoke. I met him through his wife, who was more inclined toward and interested in the faith than he was. Being the amazing man and husband he was, he wasn't going to get in the way of her pursuits and even attended church with her from time to time. He was a good man, a good father, and a good cop, but he was spiritually skeptical. Police officers often witness people in their darkest, most gut-wrenching moments. They store all that up internally with few outlets. Then they come to church and hear about the goodness of God, how God has a plan, and how all things work to the good of those who believe in God. They think, *Well, this preacher hasn't seen what I've seen.*

This man, like many of us, was confronting the problem of evil and suffering in this world—what we church people call *theodicy.* His hope for humanity was skewed. He said, "When you show up on a call only to find Mom strung out in the living room, in a house that wasn't even fit for human living, and find young kids locked in a closet in their own feces, you wonder if there really is a God." Again, no canned answers or pat approaches would work here. We sat in it. We waded through it. I asked him questions. We became friends. He wanted answers, but not to questions he wasn't asking. That's the problem when we aren't curious and people-obsessed. We give answers that fly past the person because that's not what they are asking. We wrestled with a world gone awry, the sinfulness of humanity, and the vulnerability of God at the cross in the person of Jesus. We talked of God's tenacious pursuit of humanity, even amid the most startling depravity. The connection to faith must be consistent to the quest of the individual. I had the privilege of baptizing him as he affirmed his public commitment to his faith.

A Drug Dealer

The entire time we sat for coffee, he was edgy. He wanted to talk faith, but he was waiting for his direct report. He was a mid-level drug dealer, and his boss would be coming by for some accounting, accounts payables, and distribution concerns. He said to me, "When the truck pulls up, I'm going to get in. We will be driving around the backside of that building. You need to not pay attention. When I'm done, I'll be back."

There's a first time for everything. We talked about Jesus and faith. I had been introduced to him through a common friend. My conversion story piqued his interest. As we were talking, the truck rolled up, and everything went down just as he instructed. I sat, nursed my coffee, read, and waited. He returned, shaken but content to stay engaged. (I guess his performance review didn't go well.)

He said to me, "If I'm going to do this Jesus thing, it's going to cost me—I mean, *really* cost me. It could put my life in danger."

I asked him if he wanted to pray to say yes to Jesus.

He laughed. "Jeff, I'm not there. I know the moment I take this step, I have to be committed to seeing it all the way. I'll have to give up some things. I'll have to be prepared for the consequences. I'm not there."

So we met, often. We became friends. He started attending church, searching out other employment opportunities. Slowly he moved closer and closer to Jesus. Pie-in-the-sky and sweet-by-and-by theology would not cut it. The Romans Road to Salvation wasn't compelling. He knew he was a sinner, that he'd cornered the market on depravity, and that he wasn't *waiting* for hell—he lived there already, and created it for others. What his story required was a new Lord, a new allegiance, a shift. He had to know what this leap would mean, and that it would be worth it. Did the story of Jesus hold water? Was there something to it? Was it worth what it might cost? I met him with curiosity, commitment, compassion, candor, and an eventual invitation to be an apprentice of Jesus. I eventually had the privilege of baptizing him.

Each of these stories illustrates that the truth of the story of Jesus must be woven into the uniqueness of each person's individual story. We only arrive at this point by being deeply committed to learn, listen, and love, remaining people-obsessed and insatiably curious. This posture is in sync with what we witness throughout Scripture.

Reading the Room

Our evangelism methodologies have often been shaped by the assumptions of reductionism: let's reduce all this down to the smallest common unit and go forward from there. Reductionism strips people's lives of intricacy. It treats people as a homogenous mass. It might produce results, but it often fails to lead to a deep, personal, organic transformation—not to mention it is at odds with the story of Scripture. The New Testament paints a picture of the good news mattering in a variety of different contexts among a variety of different people in beautifully organic ways. Not everyone we bump into will have the same story, the same needs, or the same questions. Not every person is searching for the same thing. Scripture points to a plurality of seekers.

The Late-Night Cynic

"He came to Jesus at night . . ." (John 3:2). I love the specific details that are provided in the stories of the gospel. Nicodemus—a member of the religious ruling class of ancient Israel, who would have a lot at stake in maintaining a public image of decorum and toeing the party line—couldn't leave well enough alone. There was something about Jesus that was so extraordinary it had created a pull. Nicodemus seemed to acknowledge there was something to this whole Jesus thing, but he wasn't certain as to what that something was. He wanted to know more, so he sought out Jesus under the cover of darkness.

For many cynics and skeptics, darkness is where the search begins—along the edges, out of sight of their friends, fearing they will be seen as sellouts. They arrive with questions and doubts, looking for a receptive ear, a presence that isn't easily threatened, one that can hear their hearts but offer meaningful responses. They know there will be a cost. Jesus doesn't hide this reality. He leans in with the recognition that there will come a moment when a rebirth will be required, a coming out of the dark and into the open.

Is This Credible?

"Are you the one who is to come, or should we expect someone else?" (Luke 7:19). Facing the uncertainty of his demise, John the Baptizer and his followers wanted to ensure that what was unfolding before their eyes was credible. Was it worth putting their hope in? Was this the *something* that would make whatever came next worthwhile? There are many seekers—those who assume there is more to life than what they are currently experiencing—but they don't want a religion that is nothing but hype and propaganda, smoke and mirrors. They are looking for something with substance, something that can hold water, something that has the stability of a foundation that will remain steady when the storms of life roll in.

In chapter 8, we will examine the necessity of a credible witness. Many are watching the church to see if what we believe is worth giving their lives to. They understand the cost it will mean for their lives. When we act contrary to Christ, it calls our credibility into question. I love how Jesus answered John's disciples: "Go back and report to John what you have seen and heard: The blind receive sight, the lame walk, those who have leprosy are cleansed, the deaf hear, the dead are raised, and the good news is proclaimed to the poor" (Luke 7:22). Jesus essentially said, *the proof is in the pudding*. Credibility is best demonstrated, not simply articulated. Our public performance of faith is often the means by which some watching will determine the credibility of our faith.

Shrouded in Shame

"How can you ask me for a drink?" (John 4:9). The seeking of some is hindered by the veil of shame that shrouds their lives. When Jesus set up camp in the wrong place among the wrong kind of people, it didn't take long for his life to collide with that of a woman who had worked especially hard to avoid open-air collisions. She was averse to public vulnerability. But that's the way it is with some. Their lives have left them deeply wounded and self-conscious. They've been hurt, betrayed, traumatized. The thought that there might be "good news" is lost on them. That's something for others, not for them. They deflect questions, hide behind excuses, and contrive ways to stay out of sight. They might consent to a canned approach if it will get you to move on so they can hide again. Good newsing the ashamed is a patient witness that sets up camp in their space and consistently affirms that they matter.

It takes time because they might shut down, avoid your calls, or attempt to push you away. They are open to a type of good news that can relieve the misery—they just aren't sure it exists. To good-news a person who lives in shame requires a love that debunks the self-loathing stories they tell themselves. Such a love will trump a theological discourse on salvation. They need the experience of consistent presence, patience, and love before they can believe they might be lovable by God.

Openly Ignorant

"'How can I [understand what I am reading],' he said, 'unless someone explains it to me?'" (Acts 8:31). One of the tragedies of evangelism is when we treat everyone like the Ethiopian eunuch, assuming everyone is open and just needs a little encouragement and knowledge to seal the deal. Many canned approaches begin with this assumption. We must realize that these assumptions don't prove true in a consistently post-Christianizing and secularizing world. Some people have no base. A little dollop of added knowledge will only add to their confusion.

However, some *are* already inclined, or have a faith background, or know a little bit, or are culturally Christian even if not confessionally so. They understand some elements but need someone to help them connect the dots. They are likely to show up at opportunities to learn, will ask questions, and are willing to acknowledge the gaps in their learning. Good newsers need to be able to identify those who have the bits and pieces so we can demonstrate the narrative arc of the scriptural story, the good-making of God's world, and the invitation to each of us to confessionally join this good-making work.

The Moral Example

"He and all his family were devout and God-fearing; he gave generously to those in need and prayed to God regularly" (Acts 10:2). One needn't be a Christian to be a moral person. Morality and holiness aren't always the same thing. Holiness should up the ante of our morality, but holiness is the work of God's Spirit in us. Morality is often an exercise of our will toward goodness. I've encountered people outside the faith who are genuinely more moral individuals than some I've met inside the church.

I know of a lot of good people who would not cross the threshold of a church on a Sunday morning. Some, like Cornelius, even have a proclivity to faith, living out a religious devotion without having it rooted in the specific story of Jesus. They are inclined to the things of goodness and God even if they haven't connected that inclination to Jesus. For these people, a canned approach would need to work hard to convince them of their depravity before we could make any headway. It can be challenging to tell a morally upstanding person they are first and foremost an awful human being and just don't know it. I wonder if starting instead with the prevenient grace of God might be more effective, helping them see the fingerprints and faithfulness of God already at work in their lives. We invite them to recognize that their goodness is a result of God's faithfulness, and to live a life of gratitude and responsibility, honoring the One who is the origin of all goodness.

Supernaturally Convinced

"At that hour of the night the jailer took them and washed their wounds; then immediately he and all his household were baptized" (Acts 16:33). I'm not a signs-and-wonders guy. I'm not opposed to unexplainable supernatural acts that leave people scratching their heads. I'm just not one who lives in pursuit of those occurrences. Maybe it's the natural skeptic in me, but even though I'm not inclined, I also recognize there are some who are. The jailer in Acts 16 witnessed an epic event that shifted his paradigm of perception. As Paul and Silas clung to hymnic hope, a supernatural event took place that upended the normalcy of the moment. This disruption created the crack in the ground of the man's heart that would allow grace to seep in, and the dramatic event led to his conversion.

I want to be sensitive to and recognize that good newsing will on occasion take an appearance for which there is no easy explanation. These occasions aren't for the purpose of disregarding other means of communicating and embodying the good news, nor are they meant to place one group on a spiritual level that is above other groups. It's the faithful work of God to recognize that for some, evidence without easy explanation can become the entry point into a faith that will transform perception.

Intellectually Astute

"When they heard about the resurrection of the dead, some of them sneered, but others said, 'We want to hear you again on this subject'" (Acts 17:32). I love this story of Paul in Athens. What he does in that environment is nothing short of miraculous in my mind. Paul—a Roman Jew who was trained on both the Hebrew Scriptures and Greco-Roman philosophy—had the capacity to move between spaces in a way that someone like Peter might have struggled to imitate. I'm inclined to believe that's why God dispatched Paul into some of the settings where he went. Paul understood what was at stake amid the various worldviews.

In Athens, Paul found himself in a group of intellectual elites, being formally questioned about the faith he was preaching to the people. Instead of telling them that they were so intellectually arrogant they wouldn't understand, Paul spoke their language, delivering a response that was fluent in Epicurean and Stoic philosophies, wrapping the story of God in a language they could understand. He didn't run from the intellectual challenge—he embraced it. Instead of demonizing those who head down the path of intellectualism, I wonder if we might instead believe that God raises up those who are willing to camp out in those spaces, those who love a good debate, are interested in philosophical nuances, and can speak a language that those inclined to academic interests can understand. Who knows? Such fluency might lead to the conversion of people like Dionysius, who later became one of the formal leaders of the early church.

•••

Being a faithful good newser demands a people-obsessed, insatiably curious willingness to set up shop in the peculiarity of a person's life for the sake of listening to, learning from, and loving on each person in a way that respects and affirms their dignity. It requires the patience to connect God's story with the beauty of their unique stories.

SECTION 3
Can I Get a Witness?

*And whatever you do, whether in word or deed,
do it all in the name of the Lord Jesus, giving thanks
to God the Father through him.*
—Colossians 3:17

Perhaps the most extraordinary act of mission and obedience is to
stay in your ordinary house and work in your ordinary job in the
name of Jesus. If your imagination is grabbed by being a sent people,
you will see all your life as mission.[1]

•·······················•

"Everyone knows Lauren. We can't believe he's no longer here!"

I wish I had a dollar for every time I heard those words spoken
of my predecessor in Chicago. Chicago is a big city, but I'm still
astounded by the number of people I meet, from all walks of life,
who knew Lauren. In 2013 he and his wife, Kourtney, moved
to the city of Chicago alongside several other couples to launch

---

1. Kim Hammond and Darren Cronshaw, *Sentness: Six Postures of Missional Christians* (Downers Grove, IL: IVP Books, 2014), 54.

Reach77, a ministry with a vision of impacting the seventy-seven neighborhood areas of Chicago in redemptive ways. They didn't set about to plant large, thriving churches or throw scads of money into building programs. Instead, these disciples simply sought to move into a variety of neighborhoods—Hyde Park and Greenwood on the Southside, Lincoln Park and Rogers Park on the Northside—set up camp, and build meaningful relationships with their neighbors. They weren't interested in launching ministries and endeavors that would be irrelevant to the communities. They had a common vision: to bear witness in faithful and incarnational ways in the communities where they lived.

They sought to bear witness, taking their cues from Jesus's instructions to the disciples: "But you will receive power when the Holy Spirit comes on you; and you will be my witnesses in Jerusalem, and in all Judea and Samaria, and to the ends of the earth" (Acts 1:8). Upon the dispatch of the Spirit, the church is sent out as representatives of this new kingdom and this new Lord. Their lives—the way they treated one another as well as those disconnected from the story of Jesus—were recognized as *different*. They understood they were not their own. Their commitment to Jesus meant a call to bear witness to the good news. The book of Acts is the narrative of this call. In going out— wherever they went, to whomever they went, and for whatever reason they were going—they believed God was directing their steps and calling them to present God to others faithfully, not just in words but in action.

These families of Reach77 lived in homes alongside neighbors, took responsibility for the geographic swaths of land where God had located them, partnered with nonprofit ministries, got to know the community leaders, and built beautiful networks of relationships throughout the city. In many ways, they embodied what Jay Pathak and Dave Runyon describe in their book *The Art of Neighboring*: "The solutions to the problems in our neighborhoods aren't ultimately found in the government, police, or schools or in getting more people to go to church. The solutions lie with us. It's within our power to become good neighbors, to care for the people around us, and to be cared for by the people around us."[2] Each of these families left its mark on their communities and in the lives of their neighbors. Good newsing is first and foremost the work of bearing witness.

Evangelism disconnected from witness moves too quickly toward confrontation (*Are you saved?*) and away from connection (*Can I be your friend?*). Lauren spent the better part of a decade committed to this vision. In many ways, he embodied much of what we've described in this book. Lauren and Kourtney made their neighborhood home. They committed to get to know their neighbors. They rarely drove when they moved throughout the city so they could be in proximity to people as often as possible. Lauren has a way about him. He's engaging, easy to talk to, brilliant, and able to converse with anyone from nearly any walk of life. Growing up as a missionary kid in West Africa, he was accustomed to moving through the kinds of cultural differences that so often disrupt the rest of us. He's a natural networker and collaborator. He had relationships forged with leaders in nonprofits all throughout the city. He'd sit with non-Christian business

---

2. Jay Pathak and Dave Runyon, *The Art of Neighboring: Building Genuine Relationships Right Outside Your Door* (Grand Rapids: Baker Books, 2012), 22.

owners and, by the end of their conversation, have them agreeing to donate to support a local ministry or nonprofit.

Lauren also forged meaningful relationships with refugee communities in the city, taking car seats to new parents when they learned the hospital wouldn't allow them to take their newborn child home in a car without a car seat. They took survivors of human trafficking shopping for household goods after they'd been rescued and set up in a suitable living space. Lauren found himself embedded in a predominantly Muslim community where, because of his consistent presence, kindness, empathy, and servant-like spirit, they eventually invited him to share with them the good news of the gospel of Jesus. Lauren baptized Muslims in Lake Michigan.

Lauren embodied what I would call a compelling witness. In the twenty-first century, our methods of evangelism and church that have worked in the past no longer gain the ground they once had. This reality doesn't invalidate all previous forms and methods. Instead, it reminds us that the assumptions we once made can no longer be made. Our practices change to meet the demands of the times. At a time when people have become increasingly cynical about the Christian faith, when they no longer share the vocabulary of faith, and when their worldview makes them less prone to discuss the things of God, this world needs less boisterous declaration and evangelistic bravado and more kenotic servants living emptied out for the sake of their neighbors. The nice thing is, anyone can do this! Anyone can bear a compelling witness.

In Philippians 2, Jesus is described in terms of "kenosis," an emptying out: "Who, being in very nature God, did not consider equality with God something to be used to his own advantage; rather, he made himself nothing by taking the very nature of a servant, being made in human likeness. And being found in appearance as a man, he humbled himself by becoming obedient to death—even death on a cross!" (vv. 6–8). Jesus doesn't allow the presumption of his divinity to strip him of his vulnerability and humility. He empties himself out for the sake of others. Being a compelling witness means "having the same mindset as Christ Jesus" (v. 5). Jesus demonstrates the self-giving, holy love of God. The attractiveness of Jesus's life was his consistent, credible reflection of divine intent. Being a citizen of the kingdom of God looks like hanging out with the lowliest of the low, calling tax collectors and prostitutes friends and beloved. It looks like courage in the face of corrupt powers. It looks like challenging unjust systems through both prophetic word *and* action. It means the willingness to go the extra mile, serve up the other cheek, suffer unfair accusation, and offer peace and forgiveness. Being a compelling witness means the incontrovertible evidence of God's love for all!

Lauren and Kourtney and the other families didn't move to Chicago to make a name for themselves but to make Christ's name known. They didn't seek to get things done, get people saved, and get churches built. They showed up to connect with those near to them, to offer themselves in service to their community, and to bear witness to God's good order in this world. They came to bear witness to and point others toward the kingdom. They believed that if you live compellingly enough, consistently enough, patiently enough, credibly enough, and just enough, people will stop and ask, "What's your deal?" Though they never constructed a building or launched a branded entity we would call a church, the families of Reach77 had many redemptive conversations with their neighbors, forging connections, collaborating regularly, and offering compelling witness. Driven by the good news of Jesus, they regularly made the "as you are going" commitment, leveraging their lives, their work, their networks, their influence, and their finances for the sake of the kingdom of God.

To live as a witness is to live as one who both recognizes what has been accomplished through the person of Jesus and faithfully acts in representation of that accomplishment. Witnessing is not about simply offering a canned spiel about salvation. It's about living in the open. It's about living vulnerably. It's about living as a blessing to our neighbors wherever we live, work, and play. It's about the consistent demonstration of God's grace and kindness. It's about taking a holistic approach to the care of others. It means recognizing that people aren't merely souls locked in the prison of their bodies. They are whole persons, with wants, needs, fears, and aspirations. They suffer trauma and find themselves caught up in unfair and unjust systems. They are sometimes hungry and other times exorbitantly wealthy and still incomplete. Being a witness means setting up camp, moving in, staying steady, and staying true. Our witness ultimately earns us the privilege of sharing the good news of Jesus with others.

Having laid the groundwork for good newsing, articulated its theology, and discussed the priority of ensuring that people and place matter, we now turn our attention to the work of good newsing, first demonstrated in the commitment to witness.

seven

PATIENT WITNESS

Here is a trustworthy saying that deserves full acceptance: Christ Jesus came into the world to save sinners—of whom I am the worst. But for that very reason I was shown mercy so that in me, the worst of sinners, Christ Jesus might display his immense patience as an example for those who would believe in him and receive eternal life. Now to the King eternal, immortal, invisible, the only God, be honor and glory for ever and ever. Amen.

—1 Timothy 1:15–17

We draw people to Christ not by loudly discrediting what they believe, by telling them how wrong they are and how right we are, but by showing them a light that is so lovely that they want with all their hearts to know the source of it.[1]

---

1. Madeleine L'Engle, *Walking on Water: Reflections on Faith & Art* (New York: Crown Publishing, 2016), 199.

There are moments when even the most cynical among us is forced to pause and ask, "What is happening here? This never happens!" Ben and Amy caused those moments for my wife and me.

When my wife and I met, we were both raging alcoholic clubbers who, in our early twenties, thought it would be a great idea to join together two dysfunctional people in a functional relationship called marriage. You can imagine how well that went. We got married in a religious ceremony with a preacher who prayed over us. I was fresh off the heels of resolute atheism but, thanks to a praying grandmother, dialed it back to agnosticism. My wife was raised in a family with a Catholic background but grew up knowing nothing of church, Jesus, or faith. It wasn't on our radar. Graduating from college with an English literature degree and no teaching certificate, I decided that perhaps the U.S. Army had a spot for me. Not surprisingly, they did. Within four months, I'd enlisted in the military, graduated from college, gotten married, and was sitting at the Military Entrance Processing (MEP) station preparing to be shipped off to basic training.

My new wife and I were as prepared as two people who had done little homework and failed to ask any meaningful questions. We were blindsided when we realized how long our separation from each other could possibly be. When the weight of it hit my wife, she lost it. A gracious-hearted young woman named Amy was also in the MEP station, preparing to ship her own husband off. Amy comforted my wife, and they exchanged phone numbers. Her husband, Ben, and I flew out together to Fort Leonard Wood. When we arrived and began being shuffled through the process, I kept landing in places with Ben. We were in the same group awaiting our assignment. Then we were sent to the same company for basic training. My wife and Amy stayed in touch. Ben classified as the same job I had, linguist. Neither of us knew what language we'd be assigned. Toward the end of basic training, we got our language codes, and we were both assigned Arabic. We'd be shipping off to the Defense Language Institute in Monterey, California, together to study Arabic for a year and a half. There, Angie and I and Ben and Amy would be reunited. They moved just down the road from us.

Ben and Amy were devout followers of Jesus. They didn't flaunt their faith, but there was firm conviction and holy boldness to speak about it in a setting where it would have been easier and relationally safer to just let it be. I, cynic and skeptic that I was, wasn't always supportive of Ben's faith. I'd tease, poke at him, tempt him. I wasn't a friend to saints, but Ben, thank goodness, was a friend to sinners. I'll spare you the details, but my wife and I were a hot mess! We lived a disastrously dysfunctional life. Ben and Amy camped out in our lives and wouldn't move. They were there when things blew and fell apart. Their son was born within a couple days of ours at the same hospital. Ben and Amy were patient with us. They loved us. They bore compelling witness to their faith even though I had no interest in it.

After a year and a half in California, Ben and I were shipped to Texas and our wives sent to their respective homes with kids in tow. Ben and I were together for a few months before he left for Arizona and I stayed for my first of two back surgeries. In the fall Ben and I found ourselves sent to the same duty station and same platoon. This never happens! Lo and behold, Ben and

I found ourselves on the same team preparing for deployment to the Balkans. Ben and Amy just wouldn't leave us alone. They were everywhere we were. And they camped out. They loved us. Put up with us. Cared about us. Prayed for us. They were compelling, imperfect witnesses to the grace of God.

While deployed, Ben and I lived next door to each other. On deployment, Angie's and my marital dysfunction reached its peak. Things had fallen apart back in Clarksville, and I was coming unwound in Kosovo. I remember going to Ben sheepishly and asking him to pray for me. This is the same guy I'd teased relentlessly about his faith, mocked, and tried to tempt to sin. I sat on the edge of his bed as he prayed for me. Then we found out that, due to his wife's impending delivery date, Ben would be sent home from Kosovo three months early.

About three weeks later I would experience the transformative encounter with Jesus in Macedonia that I described in chapter 5. A month after that, back in the States, my wife went through a horrific occurrence and found herself broken. Who was there to protect her, watch over her, fight for her, and take her to the office of the man who would later become my pastor, the man who would lead my wife to Jesus? Ben. Four years later Ben and Amy were still there, even though they had every reason not to be. They had camped out, cared for us, put up with our antics, and prevailed in self-giving, holy love. Ben and Amy were compelling, patient witnesses to the grace, mercy, and kindness of Jesus.

After our salvation and my return from deployment, Ben and Amy would walk closely with us for months. They were there as Angie and I came to terms with all the ways we'd hurt and wounded each other. They were there to walk with us, disciple us, and encourage us. Ben and Amy remained a strategic part of our journey of faith until life finally sent us in different directions. Ben and Amy understood something critical about being good newsers: they were *patient*, compelling witnesses who remained convinced that God had placed them in our lives and us in theirs.

Results Driven

The West is often understood within the binary context as a culture committed to doing versus being. I understand that the West is not a monolith and that not all cultures even in the U.S. are the same, but one of the major challenges for good newsing in the U.S. context is our results-driven attitude. We want to see the *immediate* fruit of our labor. If we had a mantra, it would be, "I ain't got time for that." We are not a patient people. We want everything, and we want it quickly.

In many church settings, ministry success is measured by the rate of growth—the speed with which churches can demonstrate effectiveness. We have magazines that track the fastest-growing churches. This results-driven emphasis often has churches targeting the low-hanging fruit in their communities: disenfranchised believers who've left church, are leaving church, or are culturally inclined to seek out a church. We build programs to cater to the needs of people and measure our effectiveness by how many people immediately show up. Pastors are let go for not growing their churches fast enough. All I can say is that I'm thankful Ben and Amy weren't professional

Christians, or they might not have taken time with us. They might not have been patient.

I am increasingly convinced that one of the key virtues of a twenty-first-century good newser is the willingness to commit to patience in the face of evidence that might discourage. Patience is a fruit of God's Spirit and connects us to the heart of God. Peter writes in his second letter to the churches: "The Lord is not slow in keeping his promise, as some understand slowness. Instead he is patient with you, not wanting anyone to perish, but everyone to come to repentance" (2 Peter 3:9). The Lord is patient. The Lord's love is steady and committed, not easily deterred but tenacious. It's a love that can be counted on even when some attempt to discredit it. It's the kind of love that forges a way forward even when the path seems laden with potholes and treacherous terrain. The Lord doesn't rush us to a decision or commitment. The Lord camps out in our presence, slowly drawing and wooing us according to his Spirit, drawing us even when we remain distant, wooing us even while we wander away. The Lord is steadfast even in our obstinacy. The Lord's feelings aren't easily hurt, nor does rejection leave God sulking, bruised, or insecure. The Lord is patient in his longing that we return to him and reclaim our place as co-laborers in God's good-making of this world.

Longevity of care, compassion, empathy, and friendship are necessary in a world where people are often inclined to relational cost-benefit analysis and quick departures with little explanation. That's really what is at stake in patience. Just as God was and is for us, we are for them. We are often surprised when that commitment isn't met with the kind of embrace we'd imagine, but people aren't used to being loved unconditionally. People aren't used to folks being willing to set up camp and endure. People are used to having people walk out and walk away, wanting something from them and abandoning them when they get it. People who are hurting are used to being treated like projects to fix or problems to be solved rather than people to love. When they lash out, retract, show vulnerability, or attempt to offend out of their woundedness, they expect you to leave. When you stay, camp out, and settle in, it's disruptive. Patience in the face of hurt is a compelling witness to the grace of Jesus. Evangelism that concerns itself with results ultimately ends up damaging or dismissing relationships.

Dusty Shoes and Drive-bys

But doesn't Jesus say we should wipe off the dust from our feet if we aren't received? Yes and no. Yes, he does say that. But no, he didn't intend for that statement to be used as a results-oriented copout. Dusting off feet is, for Jesus, always the last resort. It is not something to be arrived at quickly. In fact, quite the opposite. Persistence is much more indicative of the ministry of Jesus than eagerness to get up and get out. He stays in the fray even when the fray isn't kind to him.

I've witnessed too many Christians lament their lack of reception. They remind me of James and John, ready to call fire down from heaven upon the people of a Samaritan village who denied Jesus hospitality (Luke 9). Jesus just shakes his head. We really must develop a thicker skin and fortitude. When Jesus commissions the seventy-two in Luke 10, he states, "When you enter a house, first say, 'Peace to this house.' If someone who promotes peace is there, your peace will rest on them; if not, it will return to you. Stay there, eating and drinking whatever they give you, for the worker deserves his wages. Do not move around from house to house" (vv. 5–7). This passage is about the itinerant ministry of the seventy-two, but I'm struck at some of the elements present in this charge that translate in meaningful ways to the work of a good newser.

In environments that aren't openly hostile, abusive, or violently repelling, camp out. Hang out. Don't move from one place to another. Be present, especially if there are those who are open to your presence. External circumstances surrounding you might be hostile, but if you've found people among whom you might find peace and do the slow and steady work of bearing witness to the kingdom, stay. The work of building bridges, earning trust, and establishing credibility is slow and steady. This isn't something that can be done when you have one foot in and one foot out, waiting for the moment when their lack of openness will require your departure. If you aren't getting the results at the pace you hoped and you are tempted to see that as a closed door or a sign that it's time to go, they might just be testing you. Stay a little longer. Let your patience demonstrate God's persistence.

Recently I had a conversation with a friend about the need for a theology of place. We need to recognize the responsibility we have for the locations where we find ourselves. This can be a bit of a strain because some of us go to church in one community, work in another, enroll our kids in sports leagues in another, and enter into our own community long enough to pull in the garage and enter the house without being seen. This is particularly the case in suburban areas. I've found that rural communities and urban environments have a better understanding of place. There's recognition that these are my people. I live here, and I'm responsible to this place, going to the same stores, diners, cafés, and doctor offices. I pass my neighbors and may even know a few. My life in that place is representative of my patience for the people of that place. When I call a place home, I recognize the necessity of becoming entwined in the life of my community. I don't expect everything to change just because I show up or everyone to jump on my invitation to church. Instead, I take time to build relationships, make connections, field doubts, and demonstrate care in crisis.

Any dusting off of the feet is a last resort. There might come a time when it becomes evident that this group of people is so openly hostile to the good news that to persist might do more harm than good. There are moments when we plant a seed but, given the conditions of the soil or the particular nutrients of our lives, might not be able to watch it grow. We simply have to trust that we've been as faithful as we could be in that moment for that time. When we do walk away, it should be hard and not born of a martyr complex.

Another story I find to be compelling for many Christians for all the wrong reasons is Philip and the Ethiopian eunuch. Christians love this story in Acts 8. Philip is doing his "as you are going" thing when the Spirit disrupts his life and points out a seeker: "The Spirit told Philip, 'Go to that chariot and stay near it'" (v. 29). Philip is compelled to run up alongside the chariot, ask a question, hop into the man's space, share the good news, see immediate results, baptize the fella, and then be whisked away by the Spirit: "When they came up out of the water, the Spirit of the Lord suddenly took Philip away, and the eunuch did not see him again, but went on his way rejoicing" (v. 39). I call this drive-by evangelism, and we love it! There is nothing required from us other than the initial courage to run up alongside the chariot. We get to count our win. We have a good story to tell. And we aren't left to navigate the messiness that might later result.

I also love this Acts 8 story, but it is the exception and not the rule. More often it takes a good amount of time tilling the soil and discipling even as we are good-newsing. Even once someone has made a commitment to follow Jesus, the work has only just begun. Discipleship is key. If we are to take this calling to be good newsers seriously, we must commit to the time, the presence, and the patience necessary to endure the process. What if the process is the point and not merely a means to get to the point? What if we are apprenticing toward Jesus even as someone moves closer and closer to saying yes to Jesus?

eight

CREDIBLE WITNESS

In the same way, let your light shine before others, that they may see your good deeds and glorify your Father in heaven.

—*Matthew 5:16*

Evangelism isn't an intellectual or cognitive proposition detached from one's lifestyle. It's sharing the gospel born out of a gospel life—that is, a life transformed and continually shaped by the gospel. Evangelism happens when we are caught up in something bigger than ourselves.[1]

●————————●

1. Tara Beth Leach, *Radiant Church: Restoring the Credibility of Our Witness* (Downers Grove, IL: InterVarsity Press, 2021), 147.

In Search of Bad Words

"These two people are too good to be true." I remember saying this to my wife a few months after befriending Ed and Janet. When we moved to Erin, Tennessee, Ed and Janet took us in and made us family. They were the first to take us out to dinner, and they were our constant companions. Three weeks after we moved to this new pastorate and community, we lost my wife's mother unexpectedly. We went back and forth from the hospital for a week, coming home late in the evenings to find a meal from Janet waiting for us on the stove (not to mention many other dishes from other amazing human beings).

Every Thursday, Ed and I traveled around the community to go "calling." We visited some of the elderly members of the congregation, the homebound, and anyone else in the community whom Ed thought a visit from the pastor might help. Ed and Janet were there every time the church opened, and they worked alongside me to make sure it was closed up properly after services and events. People in the church loved them. People in the community loved them. I loved them!

But at one point, I thought, *Okay, this is too good to be true*. So, I set out on a covert mission to get to the bottom of things. We lived in a small community of the kind where everyone knows everyone, where someone's aunt is another person's teacher and another person's ex-spouse. The social network of that community was complicated. When I wasn't traveling around with Ed or putting on weight because of Janet's banana pudding, I'd stop into stores and diners around town. At some point, I might drop Ed and Janet's names, saying something like, "I was eating lunch with Ed and Janet yesterday . . ." And I'd wait to see the reaction.

A look of gratitude would come across the person's face, and they would say something like, "Oh, I had Ms. Janet as a teacher, and my child did as well! She was so kind to me. Though we didn't have much, she made sure we had what we needed."

Or they might say, "Oh, Ed! My granny was down sick for a while, and Ed would just stop by and mow her lawn and not think twice about it."

Constantly, Ed and Janet were lauded with praise, with the consistent refrain, "I thank God for them." I couldn't find anyone to say anything bad about them.

Now, that's not to say they were perfect. None of us are. Ed was particular. He liked everything a certain way. But he was never one to point out an error without a willingness to get into the mix and help someone figure it out. He was a shrewd negotiator and would hold a vendor's feet to the fire. He owned his own carpet-cleaning business and had high standards regarding business conduct and ethics. Janet was a schoolteacher for thirty years, and her students were her mission from Jesus. She had a keen understanding of theology of place, even though she wouldn't have used those words. She showed up, day in and day out, camped out, and loved those kids with the fierce, unrelenting love of Jesus.

There is no telling the number of people Ed and Janet impacted for the kingdom of God through their steady, faithful, compelling, patient, *credible* witness. Credibility marks the life of the person whose confession of faith is always preceded by their demonstration of faith. Put plainly, they walk the walk and don't just talk the talk.

Cheap Knock-Offs

Two of the watches I own have nice brand names on them, but I'm pretty sure they aren't genuine. They mostly look the part, but there are things that don't add up when you dig a little deeper. I got one as a great deal on Amazon. I was stoked. I saved hundreds of dollars. When it arrived, I loved it, and I went to register it for the warranty. When I plugged in the numbers on the website, there was no record this company had ever made this watch.

We live in a culture of knock-offs and scams. Many things look too good to be true, and often they are. Pictures are doctored, filtered, and made to appear different than the original. This is the world we live in, and people are particularly guarded against being duped. They want the real deal. Cheap knock-offs won't cut it. When I speak with young people, this is one of the dominant motifs that bubbles to the surface when we talk about faith and religion. The interactions they've had haven't always been positive. Too often, they've watched people claim one thing and embody another. This disconnect is a hindrance to good newsing. People don't find good news in hypocrisy. They are apprehensive, wondering when the too-good-to-be-true will be revealed for what it really is.

Christians seeking to live out the good news will need to commit to credibility. A credible witness is an authentic representative of the message in their authenticity, actions, attitudes, relationships, and vulnerability. They live with a constant sense of responsibility, recognizing that, wherever they go, people are watching. They recognize that just because they could doesn't mean they should. I'm reminded of the apostle Paul: "'All things are permitted,' but not all things are beneficial. 'All things are permitted,' but not all things build up" (1 Corinthians 10:23, NRSVUE). Credible good newsers are cognizant that the only evidence some people will have of God is what is witnessed in their lives. This is not something they run from, but instead they embrace it as an opportunity to be stewarded. They are not inauthentic in this pursuit but seem to live in beautiful fusion with the Holy Spirit.

Good newsers understand the truth that credibility is earned over time and lost in a moment. Credibility is rooted in our patience, persistence, and consistency. People watch. They listen. They observe and, over time, decide if we can be trusted. Credibility isn't established in controlled environments where it's easy to put on the façade of faith. Credibility is established when we are placed under pressure, in those moments when it's not as apparent how many are watching, when our vulnerability reveals what is truly at the core of who we are. Credibility is recognized not in the grand declarations but in the small, steady, faithful actions of care and kindness, of compassion and empathy, of showing up and leaning in, of loving well and indiscriminately. Over time, we earn the trust of others. They begin to glimpse in our lives the genuine expression of the kingdom, recognizing in us something different. They've come to know the difference between pretenders and those whose faith has formed them to be deeply virtuous and compelling people.

But, just as credibility is earned over time, it can also be lost in an instant. Is that fair? Not always, but people are looking for reasons not to believe. I once attended a high school basketball game and said hi to several of the people who attended my church. After the game, a random person came up to me and said, "Preacher, can you come to the basketball games more often? Some of your people behave themselves better when you're here." I had only known these people in controlled environments. Put a little pressure on them, and their credibility was lost. I've witnessed the same phenomenon on social media. The times Christians have told me, "I should be able to say whatever I want—it's a free country" have left me thinking, *Everything is permissible, but not everything is beneficial.* When Christians rant on social media, although we may believe we have the "right" to do it, such behavior may have unnecessary and unfortunate implications for how we are received by others.

Credibility as a good newser is never just about one person. It's reflective of the people to whom we belong. Our witness is tied to the broader understanding of how people perceive and receive the church—the people of God. Tara Beth Leach suggests the following: "Our witness is corporate, found within congregations and communities. Our witness is collective presence and voice and light rather than individuals."[2] When we betray our calling by acting like cheap knock-offs—good enough to pass unexamined but under pressure or scrutiny revealed to be fake—we reflect poorly on God's church. If we find ourselves belonging to a group of people whose actions and attitudes are

2. Leach, *Radiant Church*, 22.

known throughout the community to be toxic, judgmental, or hypocritical, that will be reflected in our credibility as well. We are in this together.

So You Mean Holiness?

We actually have a word for credibility in the church, and that word is *holiness*. I'm convinced that what makes the church credible in our witness of good news to the world around us is holiness. Holiness, when understood within the scope of the biblical story, should posture the church as a gift to the world. Before attempting to understand how, we first need to note what we don't mean. Holiness can be a convoluted word that carries a connotation that is less gift and more burden.

To some, holiness can mean a rigorous adherence to a rigid and narrow set of rules and expectations. This view of holiness, otherwise known as legalism, is about the performance of Christianity on the back of our moral will to do what we "ought" to do. Unfortunately, in this view of holiness, the "ought" isn't usually defined. Instead, what tends to be defined is what we ought *not* do. People who don't live up to the standard are considered "unholy." Legalism sets people apart from others based on a growing sense of self-righteousness. It's weighty and cumbersome, often judgmental and condemnatory. It has the appearance of strict obedience to Jesus but leaves the deeper elements of life untouched.

For others, holiness is rooted in the idea of a remnant church that is at war with the world around it. This kind of holiness is defined by a clear expression of discontent with the persistent slide of society into perversity. Any collaboration with those who are not like us is complicity with the enemy. There's no recognition of the beauty of the world or of those who seek God's goodness outside the church.

These flawed expressions of holiness are not a gift to the world. They are a threat to the church's credibility, and they betray our witness as good newsers. Holiness that is a gift to the world comes to the world through the Spirit of God, manifest in the people of God—who, in dying to themselves, are made alive in Christ. Holiness as a gift and as an establishment of credibility is a life lived in beautiful fusion with the Holy Spirit as the church is formed to be an alternative people. Holiness as credibility prioritizes love. Love sets the standard for all conduct. This love is reflective of a life filled up and flowing over with the goodness and grace of God at work in the people of God.

This holiness is reflected in a Christlikeness that is made possible through the Spirit. It takes seriously the entirety of Jesus's life. The church takes its cue from the One who comes low and makes himself vulnerable to those to whom he is sent, without presumption or superiority. The church recognizes that life is best lived "eucharistically," meaning that the church is taken into the hands of God, blessed, broken, and given to the world. The church isn't militant. The church is servant. The church, as good newsers, puts on full display a fruit that it could not produce of itself, especially when placed under pressure.

The church lives in light of the resurrection and the proclamation of the kingdom, recognizing that this world is destined for good—a project to which we give our whole selves. This is the holiness that refuses the swagger of self-righteousness and instead is inclined toward humility. This holiness feeds the hungry, clothes the naked, comforts the grieving, welcomes the left-outs, and befriends the unloved. It doesn't do so as a program or demonstration of self-congratulation but as that which is natural to its being in the world. Holiness as the work of the Spirit in the church is evidence of the life of Jesus to the glory of the Father. This is the kind of holiness that is a gift to the world.

Peeking behind the Curtain

Credibility in the twenty-first century does not mean we have untarnished armor, flawless stories, or invulnerability. The watching world does not demand good newsers to embody perfectionism. The world simply seeks sincerity, authenticity, and vulnerability. They are looking for a glimpse behind the curtain of Christian image.

Credibility means holy consistency and Spirit-filled, virtuous action. However, it also means that good newsers are courageous enough to live in the open. They admit, confess, and seek urgent remedy for the moments they've veered off course from what they sought to embody. Credibility is about refusing to hide the struggles of life but instead demonstrating God's faithfulness and grace *amid* the struggles, the pain, the hiccups, and the hurt that life can bring. Credibility teaches good newsers that there is no need to fill the dead space of difficult situations with glib responses and pat answers. We can sit in the difficulty and wade through inconvenience with others, fully acknowledging the challenges these difficulties mean for our faith. Speaking about Jesus is natural, not forced. There's a sincerity that marks the faith of a good newser that makes good newsers respected even if they are not agreed with.

Over the last couple of years, as evangelicalism has been caught up in the maelstrom of political division and the failure to reckon with the systemic injustices that have plagued the lives of so many, I've had conversations with my son.

He'd ask, "Is all of this real? Is there anything to this Christianity thing?"

I'd eventually respond, "Son, that's something you will have to weigh out for yourself. I can't answer that question for you. You have witnessed the lives of people like Ed and Janet, Earl and Karen, Chris and Wendy, Ginger and Sandy, Robin and David, Teresa and Tommy, Bryan and Pam, Tim and Shelly, Shirley and Mack. You've seen credible demonstrations of the faith. You have to decide for yourself if that's enough."

So far, that evidence is compelling and credible. He stays. These witnesses remain bringers of good news to him.

nine

JUST
WITNESS

*The King will reply, "Truly I tell you, whatever you did for
one of the least of these brothers and sisters of mine, you
did for me."*

—*Matthew 25:40*

There should be no tension between evangelism and justice
within the body of Christ, as it's unnecessary to prioritize one
over the other. The Bible clearly does not. Both are biblical and
two sides of the same coin: proclaiming and demonstrating the
work and witness of God. To complete the God-ordained mission
of the church, you can't have evangelism without justice. There
is no fulfillment of the Great Commission without following the
first and second greatest commandments to love God and to
love your neighbor as yourself.[1]

---

1. Alvin Sanders, *Uncommon Church: Community Transformation for the Common Good* (Downers Grove, IL: InterVarsity Press, 2020), 93.

A Megachurch Gone Rogue

"We see no disconnect between our message of helping people find their way back to God and the pursuit of biblical justice as a sign of God's kingdom coming on earth as it is in heaven."

This was the clear message established by the core leadership team of Community Christian Church on the back end of what had been for them, like many others, a tumultuous year. Having navigated COVID, a year of no in-person gatherings, the racial reckoning that rippled into and through many of the communities where the church had planted their nine campuses, the shootings that continually impact the Chicagoland area, a politically divisive season, and the storming of the nation's Capitol, Community Christian Church had taken a moment to evaluate their posture toward the world around them. One might say they were doubling down on their commitment to be the kind of church that sought redemption and restoration within their communities, even as they clearly articulated an invitation into the lordship of Jesus.

I've had a peripheral relationship with Community Christian for the last few years as they have served as mentors in our vision for church planting and multiplication at Bridgeway Community Church in Pekin, Illinois. When my wife and I moved to Chicago in 2019, I reconnected with my good friend Jon, who lived in my neighborhood. Knowing that the nearest church from my own tradition was a twenty-minute commute several neighborhoods away, I had a real desire to see my neighborhood of seventy thousand as my parish. If I connected with someone who was disconnected from Jesus and they demonstrated an interest in church, I wanted to be able to connect them to a church I trusted in our own community. Community Christian had a campus in my neighborhood. I started attending three weeks before COVID and then was asked to lead a men's small group to help relieve some of the pressure Jon was feeling as the church pivoted in a substantial way. I had always admired Community Christian from a distance, but now Jon was giving me an insider view. As a professor who focuses on church planting and movement making, I recognized this as an opportunity to get a clearer picture of how a multisite megachurch operated with leaders I greatly admired.

What I didn't anticipate was the deep, reflective, honest, confessional commitment I would watch a church of their size with their reach make toward the work of restorative, biblical justice. They had already established an arm of the ministry that focused on justice. However, instead of siloing this ministry during a time of volatility, they brought it front and center, realigning leadership and partnering with other organizations to learn about and help prosper the cause of racial justice and reconciliation throughout the Chicagoland area. This is a church that had grown to eight thousand people across as many as twelve campuses.

Jon and Dave, the cofounders of Community Christian Church, sit on the board of Exponential, the largest church-planting conference in the country. Their story is marked by literally thousands of people finding their way back to God and becoming apprentices of Jesus. They declared in front of all their senior, central, and lead staff, "Our mission has not changed, and our commitment to biblical justice is undeterred." Since I was given the privilege of sitting in that room, I found myself thankful to hear a church that had the reach and influence they had—with leaders who are globally sought-after speakers, authors, and mentors to so many—clearly and unequivocally voice that there is no disconnect between the work of justice and the practice of evangelism.

Anti-Political, Vocally Political, Counter-Political

Within and among those groups who are traditionally most at home being identified as "evangelical," recent U.S. history has demonstrated the internal and theological challenges behind what we mean when we say "good news." I'm not here to dissect the political ebbs and flows or name the voices I personally agree or disagree with, but given the call for "justice" nationally and globally, it has become evident to many, both in and outside the church, that Christians have not always known where, how, and in what ways to cast our lot. The political situation in the U.S. has been messy and volatile, and it has divided congregations, rippling out to threaten the fracturing of entire denominations. Our theological confusion has given way to multiple iterations of the Christian message that are informed by U.S. politics—whether in alignment with or in contrast to— and ultimately, these postures have been missionally unhelpful to the church's good-newsing objective.

Anti-Political

From some, there has been a clear anti-political message. From the pulpit, they've avoided addressing any issue that might reflect a particular leaning toward one side or another. They think Jesus wasn't about politics. They are about getting people saved and think we are all better off staying out of the mess and above the fray.

For this crowd, conversations about justice in our world have little to no place in the church. They are only interested in God's justice, which in their minds was inclined to send us to hell had it not been for the meritorious substitution of Jesus on our behalf. "Focus on what really matters" is their mantra, and what matters to them is depopulating hell.

This approach leads to a one-dimensional understanding of salvation that is disconnected from the wholeness Jesus sought. Those who attempt to be anti-political are, with their silence, becoming complicit with systems of injustice, leaving a damaged witness and a confusing message about the "good news" of Jesus.

Vocally Political

For others, there has been a clear and vocal political message on both sides of the two-party system in the United States.

For one group, although they view the primary responsibility of the church as being a dispenser of grace and inviter into salvation, they also believe the church in the U.S. finds itself in a precarious place with a nation sliding into depravity. Opting for an end-times narrative that sees this slide as indicative of the fast-approaching final judgment, they have taken it as their responsibility to ward off the insidious forces of evil by taking a clear political stand on one side of controversial social issues. For them, justice is God's to mete out and not ours, and focusing on social justice draws people away from the heart of the gospel and the witness of the church. The unfortunate consequence of a group of Christians being vocally political on one side of the two-party system in the United States is that Christians who identify with the other side have felt compelled to be just as vocal in response, aligning themselves with the opposite party and appearing to have little to offer of their own accord except taking stances against their opponent.

Both groups see themselves as culture warriors, and they often do not think there is room for Christians to align themselves with "the other side" and still remain Christian. Both sides are willing to cut off their noses to spite their faces. They've so thoroughly aligned themselves with a form of Christianity that is informed by their chosen political parties that they have both become one-dimensional in their approach to Christian faith and salvation. For those on the right, the dominant motif of salvation of the soul and the dualism of good-versus-evil limit their imaginations. On the left, the slow and steady improvement of society and the quest for justice at the expense of confessional faith and acknowledgment of the lordship of Jesus fails to recognize the unique narrative of the already-not-yet nature of the kingdom of God.

Counter-Political

Finally, there are those who are committed to a counter-politic. For those within this posture, the idea that Jesus's message is apolitical is absurd. They suggest that Jesus wouldn't have been killed if he had come with a fluffy, feel-good message that didn't threaten the powers of the world he entered. In reality, Jesus's announcement of a kingdom that had come already and was still yet to come was good news embraced by many *and also* bad news for the powerful. This kingdom—this counter-politic to the regimes of this world—had a unique vision for the making good of all that had become bad. For this group, justice isn't a peripheral issue or a deception that distracts from the true mission of God. Instead, it is reflective of a God who is at work in this world redeeming, reconciling, and restoring the world to God's good order.

Those who find themselves identifying with this group see resonances of God's missional ambitions in the politics of this world, but they do not see this world as capable of delivering the full measure of God's goodness. They might or might not be vocally politically active, but they live loudly in the tension that none of the work is complete or even fully faithful. In this world, compromises are made. This tension ensures a prophetic distance that allows the church to critique itself as well as any and all powers that attempt to establish God's kingdom fully on earth. Justice for this group has a unique definition that is rooted in the arc of the biblical narrative, demonstrated in the person of Jesus, announced in his kingdom, and made possible through the Holy Spirit. It isn't opposed to evangelism but is bound up in evangelism.

We must explore this posture more fully.

Same Side of the Same Coin

Eric and Amy serve at Community Christian Church. Amy oversees the justice initiatives, and Eric serves as the leader of Community Freedom, the congregation's church-planting expression within facilities of incarceration.

Amy is a passionate, committed apprentice of Jesus who sees the world in its complexity, its beauty, and its brokenness. She seeks opportunities to partner, collaborate, and engage with churches and nonprofits that are committed to a biblically restorative vision of justice. Her heart beats to see redemptive change, unjust systems challenged, and societal sins confessed. She is willing to engage conversations that would make most uncomfortable, and she operates under the assumption that the good news of the kingdom of God is bound up in God restoring the world to God's self, healing the brokenhearted, caring for the vulnerable, and imagining a future that is different from the present.

Eric is a formerly incarcerated black man who moves in and through predominantly white spaces at Community Christian Church. Because of his own experience, Eric is deeply committed to seeing people whom the world has given up on find their way back to God, be transformed by the grace of Jesus, and discover wholeness and healing no matter where they are. His consistent and faithful presence at Community Christian reminds the church that conversations about race, incarceration, systemic justice, and redemption of the least, last, and lost aren't abstract concepts but have concrete implications. Eric has planted two churches inside prisons, he disciples incarcerated men, and he baptizes new followers of Jesus. Eric's heart sings when people discover the saving grace of Jesus, just as he has.

Eric and Amy aren't opposite sides of the same coin—they are the same side of the same coin. There is no internal disconnect between the work of evangelism and the work of justice. They are dancing partners that need each other. Biblical justice is about ensuring that humanity can flourish in the ways God has intended, and that individuals are afforded the dignity that is inherent in all humanity, as those bearing the image of God. When either of those principles is betrayed through unjust systems, abuses of power, political perversion, or economic alienation, good newsers recognize that reality as out of sync with God's good making of the world. Injustice is bad news and requires a response. Response to injustice through just, restorative, and distributive action bears witness to the work of God in this world. For the good newser, we get a glimpse of the kingdom when the hungry are fed or socially unjust systems are challenged, setting the stage for the proclamation of the good news. Without just witness, the church's credibility is lost. Justice is the means through which credibility is established, often making possible the proclamation of the good news and the invitation into this kingdom community called the church. It makes aligning oneself as an apprentice of Jesus far more compelling.

When the church treats the work of justice as peripheral to God's mission or as a distraction from the gospel message, we threaten the witness of the church, truncate a vision of salvation, become complicit with powers of perversion, and leave a generally bad taste in the mouths of those who are disconnected from Jesus. Good newsing takes a holistic approach to human flourishing and dignity, proclaiming the message of the One who makes possible this flourishing *as it invites* people to follow that One. They are webbed and woven together.

SECTION 4
Saying Yes, Again and Again

This is how we know what love is: Jesus Christ laid down his life for us. And we ought to lay down our lives for our brothers and sisters. If anyone has material possessions and sees a brother or sister in need but has no pity on them, how can the love of God be in that person? Dear children, let us not love with words or speech but with actions and in truth.
—1 John 3:16-18

Helping a child learn to read, providing clean drinking water, eradicating disease, creating jobs, alleviating suffering and pain, delivering health care to people, raising children to become life-enhancing adults—all of these efforts are kingdom endeavors. . . . Simply put, every good deed and expression of goodwill points to the kingdom. The pervasive presence of good reflects a breaking-in of the kingdom of God, advancing against the kingdom of antilife.[1]

●......................●

---

1. Reggie McNeal, *Kingdom Come: Why We Must Give Up Our Obsession with Fixing the Church—and What We Should Do Instead* (Carol Stream, IL: Tyndale, 2015), 44.

They Will Be My Neighbor

"They are not clients. They are not cases. They are not projects. They are neighbors."

As we stood inside the foyer of the Shepherd Community Center on the south side of Indianapolis, Allen made the point to orient our group at the outset. "How we see people matters. How we see people impacts how we treat people."

The Shepherd Community Center has existed in their neighborhood for more than thirty years. For last two-plus decades, it has been anchored and led by Jay, who is one of the most fascinating people I've ever met and one of the most resolute good newsers I've had the privilege to mentored by.

After a brief orientation, Allen led us into Jay's office, where he continued to share with us the vision of Shepherd Community. "We are not a social-service organization. That's the challenge. That's the potential drift. When you do what we do in this community, it can be tempting to view us as a dispenser of social services. However, we know the why behind what we do. That why is never disconnected from the Who that has called us to that work. We make no bones about it. We are here because of Jesus. Beyond introducing people to our services, we hope to introduce people to Jesus. We believe he is truly the good news."

Shepherd Community Center and the church connected to it operate in the second-most violent community in the city of Indianapolis. Within the square mile surrounding the church, thousands of people live under the psychological, spiritual, and physical constraints of poverty, violence, addiction, and marginalization. But that's the easy story to tell. Jay and his phenomenal team know otherwise. They know their neighbors to be resilient, creative, and loved by God. Their neighbors aren't problems to be fixed. They are people to be loved. That love takes the form of a school for children as well as adult education programs that teach healthy eating and cooking, budgeting, and parenting. It has taken the form of food distribution and a free medical clinic. It takes the form of a consistent presence, a solidarity with neighbors, where numerous staff members live in and around the neighborhood, in the ebb and flow of community dynamics. It takes the form of advocating politically for the sake of the community and leveraging the finances of the rich to build sustainability and stability programs for those without the resources. Love takes the form of seeking to change the perspective of their neighbors regarding first responders, employing both a police officer and an EMT to work on proactive community engagement. They build relationships and respond to crises in redemptive ways. It takes the form of a church that creates multiple spaces for neighbors to come, worship, and be introduced to the hope anchored and rooted in Jesus.

The Trinity of Good-Newsing

How we see people impacts how we treat people. This has been the message throughout this work. When we see the other as a "them" who needs fixing, a "them" we make a salvation project, we strip people of their dignity, turning our relationships into impatient, imprudent transactions. However, when we see the other as *us*—as our neighbors, as those we live with and alongside—our presence as good newsers will be contextually relevant to the factors that continually impact their lives. It will mean the good news isn't merely an event, formalized by a prayer; instead, it is a lifestyle lived with and among our neighbors. It will mean that justice isn't a caveat to the gospel but the real and necessary response to the needs, hurts, and pain of our neighbors. And it will mean that discipleship doesn't begin as a response to an event of salvation. Instead, discipleship will be understood as an apprenticeship to Jesus that begins when we step into the lives of others.

As we follow Jesus and live as compelling, patient, credible, just witnesses to the good news of God's redemptive designs in this world, we are inviting our neighbors to apprentice us as we apprentice Jesus. Discipleship is about modeling Christlikeness in unique contexts and among unique peoples. It is a process that is practiced and not merely the result of "classroom" time. When we value our neighbors as already loved by God, then apprenticeship may begin even before our neighbors accept the gift of grace and fully align themselves with Jesus.

Evangelism, justice, and discipleship are the trinity of good news, a holistic embodiment of a whole gospel of Jesus. In an increasingly post-Christian, often desperate context, the church's embodiment of these three is necessary to forge a way forward for God's redemptive purposes to bear meaningful fruit in the lives of our neighbors—those already loved by God, even if they aren't aware of it.

ten

WHAT
COMES *FIRST*

*Instead, we were like young children among you. Just as
a nursing mother cares for her children, so we cared for
you. Because we loved you so much, we were delighted
to share with you not only the gospel of God but our lives
as well. Surely you remember, brothers and sisters, our
toil and hardship; we worked night and day in order not
to be a burden to anyone while we preached the gospel of
God to you. You are witnesses, and so is God, of how holy,
righteous and blameless we were among you who believed.
For you know that we dealt with each of you as a father
deals with his own children, encouraging, comforting and
urging you to live lives worthy of God, who calls you into
his kingdom and glory.*

—1 Thessalonians 2:7–12

A Spiritual Nudge or Paradigm Shift?

In Christendom, there has been an assumption, whether stated or otherwise, that evangelism is the event that precedes the ongoing work of discipleship. This assumption has given birth to the corollary that evangelism as an event secures a destination even if discipleship is lacking or absent. I get the sense that the apostle Paul might disagree.

Paul was in Thessalonica for about six weeks before being chased out. He'd been there just long enough to spark an interest in Jesus that gave birth to a fledgling church made up of those who were inclined to trust that this message about a counter-kingdom and new Lord was worth pursuing. He was there just long enough to dig a foundation, and then he was forced to flee. When he writes to the church later, he confesses a deep concern he's had: "For this reason, when I could stand it no longer, I sent to find out about your faith. I was afraid that in some way the tempter had tempted you and that our labors might have been in vain" (1 Thessalonians 3:5). He was afraid that, even though his evangelism had been effective, the devil might cut in and undo all his work.

Paul was ecstatic to hear a report from his friend Timothy that God's Spirit had sustained the church even in the face of a looming threat. Evangelism without discipleship for Paul felt pointless. Paul would not have understood an "at least conversion, but hopefully some discipleship" mentality. Evangelism as bearing witness to and declaring the good news and discipleship as apprenticing toward the embrace and embodiment of good news, evidenced in continued growth in Jesus and participation in his mission, all went hand in hand.

The church in the West has mistakenly assumed one other notion, that people generally know what needs to be done and simply need a spiritual nudge to be saved, be born again, and make Jesus their personal Lord and Savior. If we can just get them somewhere where the gospel is preached, appeal to their inclination that they are sinners in need of grace, offer forgiveness through repentance, and pray a prayer, then we are off to the races! But what happens when these assumptions no longer hold? What happens if the neighbors to whom we are sent, the people we come across each and every day, have no preexistent knowledge of the story of Jesus or belief in God? What if the expanding group of "nones"—those with no religious affiliation—have little to no spiritual background from which to draw? If that's the case, then a nudge won't work. Put them in the "right" environment, and you might draw confused looks, not numerous conversions.

I am not suggesting that the supernatural work of the Spirit through the preached word to people who've never been introduced to the message of Jesus can't in some sense produce a conversion that is transformative. God is capable of things my little mind and feigned theological expertise has little way to make sense of. But operating on the assumption that people have some kind of background or past exposure to the gospel is generally poor practice. Good newsing *only* assumes the need to be present with and among others, bearing witness faithfully and regularly to the good news of Jesus, which also suggests that the work of making disciples precedes the event of evangelistic conversion. People aren't waiting for a little nudge. They are being invited into a complete paradigm shift that will require faithful, patient modeling prior to their embrace of the good news *as well as* faithful, steady, continued modeling long after that embrace has been made.

Follow Me as I Follow Jesus

In the past when I've read 1 Corinthians 11:1, I've been struck by Paul's seeming arrogance: "Follow my example, as I follow the example of Christ." I've thought, *Why wouldn't you just tell people to follow Christ?* Being a good newser has given me a fuller understanding of Paul's posture in this scripture. To tell someone to follow Jesus who has no idea who Jesus is, what following him looks like, or even the first steps to take is a fool's endeavor. Good newsers know that, as our culture becomes less familiar with Christian imagination and less inclined to the narrative of Scripture, our assumptions of readiness to follow Jesus must be modified. Those who are completely disconnected from the hope found in Jesus need those who will "example" Jesus-following, those who—being apprentices themselves—will faithfully and steadily apprentice others. This means a few things.

1. Relationships Can't Begin after Conversion

Under the old models of church, our relationship with people who didn't believe often meant just enough to invite them to church. Then, having an encounter with Jesus would lead them to be born again and would result in our increased relationship with them—now that they were one of us. Good newsers recognize how unfortunate this model is, and we don't wait for the "non-believer" to come to us. Instead, we go to our neighbors. In going to our neighbors and meeting them where they are, we begin the work of apprenticing them to Jesus by witnessing to the good news without demanding a decision or even a response from them.

2. Our Re-presentation of the Good News Matters

If we assume that our showing up begins the work of evangelism, then we recognize the importance of our witness to the good news. Remember the credible witness thing we talked about? Yep, that. In growing in our Christlikeness, we seek to embody the kind of presentation of our beliefs that models a lifestyle worth following. If there is a disconnect between belief and action, there will be a confusion about apprenticeship to Jesus.

3. They Will Be Watching

Cue the discomfort! In seeing discipleship as the work that precedes a person's embrace of Jesus, we recognize that people will be watching our conduct, our actions, our speech, and— yep—our social media presence. Many with little to no knowledge of Jesus will assume that what you do and the way you act is representative of the Jesus you say you follow. Apathy and indifference to this truth will lead people down paths that Jesus wouldn't take them. Good newsers live our lives on display. We invite people into our lives and give them a glimpse into a picture of who Jesus is.

4. Invite Them to Belong before They Believe

Discipleship that precedes the embrace of good news means discipleship isn't constrained by the limitations of classroom and curriculum. It means discipleship happens on the way. As we busy ourselves with the good work of Jesus, we invite people along with us into the redemptive work, leveraging what they've been given by God to steward for the good of others. We bring them with us into settings and environments where they can do the good that God calls them to. We follow them into settings where they are already committed to the good work of God's kingdom even if they can't, at this point, recognize the why behind what they do.

5. Reflection and Conversation along the Way

I love when people quote the cliché that is often wrongly attributed to St. Francis of Assisi: "Preach the gospel always; if necessary, use words." Sounds great, right? Unfortunately, words are often necessary because words convey meaning and frame worldviews. Demonstration without conversation is behavior modification and not paradigm transformation. As we make disciples on the way, as we bring people along and go along with them into the good work of God in this world, we learn to have meaningful, prudent, authentic conversations about why what we've done reflects God's intentions for the world. We listen intently to the kinds of questions asked, the problems voiced, the confusion confessed. Good newsing means we don't run away from connecting our actions to the *source* of our actions. Seek to reveal to those who apprentice alongside you the name of the One we apprentice—the who behind the what.

6. Don't Run from the Invitation

As we disciple on the way, apprenticing people toward Jesus even before they embrace Jesus, we ought not be surprised when the people we've walked with begin to display an interest in making their followership official. As people apprentice us as we apprentice Jesus, there may be a growing sense of God's grace and goodness in the world. There may come a time when someone seeks to make their citizenship in this new kingdom official. It might be time for a confession, a decision, a prayer, and an acknowledgment of allegiance to a new Lord. This is often the Spirit-filled bubbling to the surface of the work that has been unfolding toward that moment. We can't run from that! We must be prepared in that moment to offer an invitation into that allegiance, to embrace their inclusion, and to name Jesus as the new author of their story.

7. Don't Stop with the Embrace

A good newser doesn't get someone to the point of decision and then abandon them. When someone yields themselves to Jesus, a substantive shift will take place in their lives. Discipleship and good newsing continues long beyond the moment of yes to Jesus. In prevailing in our presence among them, we are helping them prioritize consistency in growth and the opportunity to become the kinds of people who apprentice others even as they apprentice Jesus. We call this kingdom multiplication!

eleven
KEEP IN STEP

Since we live by the Spirit, let us keep in step with the Spirit.

—Galatians 5:25

The Spirit is the agent of God to engage the reality of every cultural context with the reality of the redemptive reign of God in Christ and the church as God's new creation of community in the world.[1]

Dancing on the Toes of the Father

I love weddings. I love officiating weddings. I love seeing wedding photos on Instagram. I love everything about weddings. I'm one of those pastors who covets the opportunity to

---

1. Craig Van Gelder, *The Ministry of the Missional Church: A Community Led by the Spirit* (Grand Rapids: Baker Books, 2007), 58.

participate in such a sacred event in a person's life. One of my favorite parts of the wedding day is the reception, where I can simply sit on the edges of the action and people-watch. One of my favorite scenes to watch is, after the dance floor has been opened up to all, when a young girl will go out to dance with her daddy. She steps out onto the dance floor and then climbs up on Daddy's shoes, and his movements carry her along. It's beautiful. She knows her movements are bound up in her father's movements. The grace of the dance is located in the faithfulness of his motions. If Daddy chooses to go right but she is determined to go left, chaos will ensue. The dance requires submission to the movement.

I tend to believe that life as a good newser is similar to the dance of a little girl with Daddy. At its core, evangelism is not a method, tactic, or program. It is a deeply spiritual activity born on the shoes of our Father. It is made possible through the movement of the Spirit in and through our lives, carrying us out into the world in the beautiful dance of God. It is a dance for the sake of those whom God would carry us toward because God loves them that much. Too often, evangelism is so tac- tic-heavy and method-driven that it is devoid of sensitivity to and discernment of the Spirit. It gives no space for the dance to occur, no beautiful, subtle movements of our lives into the lives of others. Instead, with agenda in hand and a quota to meet, it hurries in, announces intent, extends invitation, and moves on in the absence of outcome. There's no listening empathetically with ears inclined to what the Spirit might share. Instead, with a canned pitch in hand, it already knows what needs to be said.

The Acts of the Spirit

The collection of stories that immediately follows the stories of the life of Jesus in Matthew, Mark, Luke, and John is called Acts of the Apostles, but sometimes I think the book would be better titled Acts of the Spirit. The Spirit of God takes center stage in this collection of stories. Without the Spirit, the apostles would have been doomed to good intentions with poor outcomes. Instead, the Spirit—as evidenced at Pentecost and consistently throughout the stories—bears a fruit that points to the faithfulness and efficacy of God through his witnesses rather than just the witnesses themselves. The Spirit is the actor. The following quotes are just from the first third of the book:

- *All of them were filled with the Holy Spirit and began to speak in other tongues as the Spirit enabled them (2:4).*
- *After they prayed, the place where they were meeting was shaken. And they were all filled with the Holy Spirit and spoke the word of God boldly (4:31).*
- *Brothers and sisters, choose seven men from among you who are known to be full of the Spirit and wisdom (6:3a).*
- *When they arrived, they prayed for the new believers there that they might receive the Holy Spirit (8:15).*
- *When they came up out of the water, the Spirit of the Lord suddenly took Phillip away, and the eunuch did not see him again, but went on his way rejoicing (8:39).*
- *Then Ananias went to the house and entered it. Placing his hands on Saul, he said, "Brother Saul, the Lord—Jesus, who appeared to you on the road as you were coming here—has sent me so that you may see again and be filled with the Holy Spirit" (9:17).*

In reading through the book of Acts, we recognize the work of the Spirit in the missional posturing of the church. The Spirit compels the followers of Jesus into precarious places, dispatches them into out-of-bounds spaces, and inclines them toward people who are initially resistant to God's good actions. The Spirit seems to prompt a spiritual discernment to see opportunities where there are closed doors and closed doors where there are assumed opportunities. The Spirit emboldens the disciples to testify about the person of Jesus and the work of redemption. The Spirit seems to create the kind of environment that is necessary for spiritual fruit to be birthed.

Good newsing is the fruit of a life lived in the Spirit of God and the missional impulses of God. Within both the Greek language (the original language of the New Testament) and the Hebrew language (the original language of the Old Testament), the word "Spirit" is translated from words that can mean "breath" and/or "wind." That means life as a good newser is caught up in the breath of God. As we know, breath has two movements—an inhale and an exhale. Being a good newser means participating in the breath of God. Through the inhale, we are drawn through our worship into the heart of God, having our ambitions, intentions, and attitudes transformed by the beauty of grace, having our perspectives changed in light of God's love, and having our rough edges sanded by God's faithful mercy. In the exhale, we are sent out redemptively into the world, bearing in our bodies the good news through which we've been transformed. The movement of inhalation and exhalation ensures that, as we are being made holy, we are also being sent missionally. Only through the overflow of our participation in God's breath have we any good news to offer others.

God Got There First

Perhaps the single most compelling theological category that had me leaning toward the Wesleyan tradition is the idea of prevenient grace—the "grace that goes before." Good newsers assume that, long before we've ever shown up in the life of someone else to bear witness to the good news, God got there first. God's grace and God's Spirit are already at work in the lives of the people we go to before we get there. Before Peter hops off the roof at Simon the Tanner's house in Acts 10 to rush to Cornelius and proclaim the good news, the Spirit was already present with Cornelius, prompting and preparing him for the encounter. God loves people that much. God doesn't wait for us to get our act together. God is already acting upon, wooing, preparing, and demonstrating faithfulness. Good newsers take great comfort and peace in the knowledge that we aren't being called to anywhere that God has not already gone.

If the Spirit of God is at work in the life of the good newser, dispatching and deploying us into the lives of others, and the Spirit of God is already at work in the lives of those we've been sent and dispatched to, that must mean the Spirit of God is actively engaged in the work of orchestrating divine collisions. Good newsers don't believe in chance encounters. Good newsers believe in divine opportunities. Good newsers are attuned to the daily encounters, the meaningful relationships, and the unique opportunities that we encounter each and every day.

Taking an Ancient Lead

The book of Acts is not meant to operate as a prescription: "Do this, and you will get this outcome." Instead, Acts should be read through the lens of missional patterning. When I think about living into the rhythm of good news evidenced by the lives of the early Jesus apprentices as they danced with the Spirit, a pattern begins to emerge for the work of evangelism in sensitivity to the Spirit of God.

Pray Fervently

Good newsers recognize that the wellspring of guidance and goodness comes from a life spent in fervent prayer for those who are disconnected from Jesus, for the pain people feel, for the consecration of our lives in service to God, for divine opportunities, and for our sensitivity to the Spirit's leading. Prayer activates discernment, learning to look into the world with the eyes and heart of Jesus. Prayer is a means of cooperating with God in God's purposes.

Care Deeply

Life in the Spirit makes us consistently discontent with the current state of affairs. It means we cannot be apathetic or indifferent to the suffering of others. It preconditions us to care. We live out of a spiritually infused empathy, where our hearts are inclined to connect to the deeper needs, sorrows, struggles, and celebrations of others. Being a good newser means we often wake in the morning bearing others upon our hearts and end the day by carrying those we've carried with us in concern throughout the day into the arms of God through prayer. Care compels us toward meaningful connection.

Listen Intently

Shut up! I once got in trouble from a seven-year-old after a service because I used those two words in my sermon. I was told, "We don't say 'shut up' in our house." I know it's not appropriate or polite, but we do have to learn to shut up. Evangelism that conditions us to speak first and listen later does a damage that I don't think we can fully understand. Good newsing prioritizes the voice of the person to whom we are sent and not our own predetermined responses. Life in the Spirit bends our ears toward others. We attend not only to what they say but also to what lies behind what they say—their fears, their hopes, their values, and their aspirations.

Watch Attentively

Pay attention. When we busily bump from thing to thing, constantly distracted by our glowing devices, our earbuds, or the ever-present schedule brimming over with demands, we will miss what we might be shown by the Spirit. Good newsers operate at a different pace with a Spirit-filled attentiveness and curiosity. One could say they are "on the lookout." *Whom might God be leading me toward today? What does that person's body language say about them?*

Speak Prudently

There will come moments along the way when we can and should speak up. However, we do so as those who make the most of every opportunity and speak in ways that are full of grace and seasoned with salt. We exercise tact in challenge. We exercise compassion in tone. We exercise restraint in explanation. We exercise humility in knowledge. I once had someone say, "You always know what to say in those moments with non-believers." No, I really don't. If a good word, a timely word, a life-giving word is spoken—it's because the Spirit of God has spoken those words through me.

Invite Boldly

I love the emboldening work of the Spirit in our lives. I can't count the number of times in my life—when I've been afforded the privilege of sharing the good news of Jesus and inviting someone into a life-changing decision—that my heart has begun to beat fast, anxiety has crept in, and I've wondered if I'm being presumptuous with what comes next. In that moment the Spirit fortifies my commitment to the good news. The Spirit emboldens us to speak a good word in the face of the timidity we might feel.

Love Fiercely

The Spirit of God produces in us a fierce commitment to love well. Good newsing is always inspired and sustained by the Spirit's work of love in and through our lives to others. In taking the Spirit's lead we are driven toward people and not away, in pursuit of connection and not in avoidance of contamination with the outside world. We step out, lean in, endure, persevere, show up again and again, and persist in our care for those God has entrusted us with, hoping they too can experience the joy and glory of living into the new story that God has made possible for all of us.

twelve
MADE
NEW

Therefore, if anyone is in Christ, the new creation has come: The old has gone, the new is here!
—*2 Corinthians 5:17*

•————————•

Dirty Water

She cussed (loudly) coming out of the water.

He did a cannonball into the baptistery.

His big ol' Harley-riding self bear-hugged me sopping wet after he took the holy plunge.

All of these are true stories. Each person experienced such a rush of emotion that they couldn't contain themselves. There was no decorum. There was no concern with being "appropriate." All there was, was a new start to an old story, with the residue of what once was left at the bottom of the sacred tank. They each entered the baptistery to bear witness to the grace extended to them, as a public witness to the yes they'd given to Jesus, as an act of association with the covenantal people of God who are committed to God's purposes in this world, and as an act of burying their old selves in the cleansing waters of God's grace. Good newsing often (though not always) leads to clear, particular, specific stories of transformation and new life. I know. I was and am one of them.

I'm going to make it short. Although I tried to be a good person throughout most of my life, I held onto atheism in my late teens and early twenties, eventually moving to agnosticism. I became a compulsive addict and binge-drinking alcoholic who married another alcoholic, which led to a catastrophic three years of marriage. Then I met Jesus, and I was *made new*.

On January 6, 2002, mere months after I said yes to Jesus, I was baptized by my pastor—the same pastor who led my wife to Jesus. Those waters meant something to me. Those waters said something about me. When we call baptism a sacrament, we are implying that there is a mystery of grace at work in those waters. I experienced that mystery. My baptism created in me a living spring, welling up and spilling out into the lives of others. I'd experienced the good news and wanted nothing more than to good-news others. I tasted of the goodness of the Lord, and I wanted to invite others to a taste test.

Early on, I was introduced to this scripture from 2 Corinthians: "Therefore, if anyone is in Christ, the new creation has come: The old has gone, the new is here! All this is from God, who reconciled us to himself through Christ and gave us the ministry of reconciliation: that God was reconciling the world to himself in Christ, not counting people's sins against them. And he has committed to us the message of reconciliation" (5:17–19). What these verses describe became both the experience of my life and my life's calling. I have given myself away to embodying the good news of being made new. I've sought to call others into the reconciled and restored relationship with the One who can make them new. Remember, God is up to something in this world, and that something God is up to is making all things new.

Fundamentally, what compels me as a good newser is my participation in that story of new things. Story after story, I've witnessed the reality of this good news. People who had played out their stories to their logical conclusions—broken-ness, desperation, despair, disappointment, purposelessness, dysfunction, and addiction—entered a life-transforming rela-tionship with Jesus. They were made new! Not only were they made new, but they also became participants in the making of all things new, in their families, at their workplaces, and in their communities. Just like the waters when the newly baptized emerge, that newness spilled out and dampened the ground around everywhere they placed their feet.

Earlier, I stated that I've sought to avoid canned presentations and methods that feel transactional. That is true. However, in the previous church I pastored, we had so many people coming to faith in Jesus and sharing their faith in Jesus with others that we needed a "way" of helping them make sense of the story. Good newsing and radical transformation became so contagious it was hard to keep up. My family ministries pastor at that church, Linsy, was a good-newsing extraordinaire! She goes where few are willing to go, to reach those few are willing to touch, to love those many are willing to leave out. In showing up and demonstrating all that has been shared thus far, she good-newsed people into the kingdom and into a yes to Jesus.

To help people derive a sense of confidence from the process, we developed a short acronym: MADE NEW. We built this acronym around the belief that the world operates under a failed story and leaves us with tried, tired, worn-out stories. The gospel is an invitation into an all-encompassing, radically transformative, new story! We become participants in the redemptive story of God at work in this world and participants in God's good-making of the world. As I conclude, I humbly leave you with a way of making sense of the movement toward the decision to embrace the good news of Jesus.

MADE NEW

M: Meet (the Storymaker, Jesus)

As noted earlier, we don't take Jesus to those who are disconnected from his hope because God's prevenient grace means Jesus is already there. Instead, we simply make the introduction. Throughout the process of apprenticing people in the way of faith, we've been discussing the origin of the goodness in which we've been participating. As someone approaches the point of their yes, I like to ensure they've been properly introduced to Jesus. I want to point out that he's been active through his Spirit all along, drawing them and preparing them for that moment. I want them to understand that the yes is to One who calls us into a particular way of living in this world and that it comes with a cost.

A: Admit (that my old story is broken, empty, and worn out)

A yes to Jesus means the transformation of our stories. At some point, each of us investigates our story and acknowledges that, outside the grace of Jesus, our stories are incomplete. For some, that will be because their stories have left them broken, disappointed, defeated. Others will have reached a pinnacle of success in the eyes of the world, tasted all the world has to offer and been left wanting. Still others long to connect their lives to something bigger than themselves. No matter where we find ourselves, there is the point of acknowledgment that the story we've been living and writing for ourselves—with "me" as the main character—isn't adequate to sustain us in the fullness of life. I confess that insufficiency.

D: Decide (to turn from the old story and embrace the new story of Jesus)

We call this *repentance*, which is much more than simply stopping the bad things we've been doing and doing the good that we should. This is a full-on perspective shift, a reorientation, a turning away from what has been and what we've known and the embrace of what is and should be. We are making a clean break with allegiances that stand in opposition to the lordship of Jesus and renouncing stories that vie for our imagination, our hopes, our passions, and our desires.

E: Embrace (the gift of forgiveness and the promise of hope and restoration)

This is the yes. The life in Christ is made up of a steady stream of yes moments, but this yes is one of embracing the good news as the constitutive story of our lives, our pursuits, and our purpose. It means we know we are no longer captive to a way of being in this world that is at odds with God's intentions. We are no longer left to wallow in the shame of our past participation. We have been rescued, redeemed, and set free. We can now pursue the One who has already been pursuing us.

N: Name (Jesus as the author of every upcoming chapter of your story)

I was once asked what the lordship of Jesus was all about. I said, "Well, you've spent the better part of your life writing your own story. Then you stumbled upon a Jesus story that is richer and more meaningful than anything you've ever written. The lordship of Jesus is about yielding your life's pen. No longer are you in charge of dictating what is to come next. You yield to Jesus every line, page, and chapter of what comes next." You have a new author.

E: Engage (Jesus daily through Word and prayer)

Because the yes is not the end but a new beginning, there is more to come. At this point I like to help people understand that their ongoing participation in the good news of Jesus is rooted in intimate relationship with Jesus. That intimacy is cultivated in and through our practices of faith, most notably getting to know him through the stories in which he chooses to reveal himself and through the fervent prayer that draws us into the life of the Spirit.

W: Walk (in obedience daily to a life of love for God and neighbor)

Finally, that yes is their initial commissioning. With a yes, they are commissioned as good newsers who are called to live in obedience to God's command to live a life of fierce love of God and neighbor. The love of God becomes the compelling force that drives them and becomes the gift through them to others.

•••

There are no magic formulas or methods that are the means through which a person gets saved. However, I've found that having a simple way to process the story of Jesus with others ensures that in the moment there is a confidence in sharing. At the end of the day, no matter how you do it, it's good news. People are made new, and all of it is a gift from God!

CONCLUSION
MORE GOOD NEWS

•——————•

There is no end to evangelism. Too often we've adopted a model of evangelism that suggests that evangelism is what *we* do to *them*. Within the context of some views of salvation, this would make sense. We (the ones who are saved) evangelize them (those who aren't). Once they say yes to Jesus, they become one of us. The only thing left then is growth in grace. But what if it isn't that simple?

What if evangelism is the ongoing work of the church in the world and *for* the church? What if evangelism is what continually places us on even ground with the world, helping us recognize that we are like them in that we are all, always in need of good news? Evangelism is the ongoing process of being good-newsed into God's kingdom vision for redemption.

Life has vulnerability embedded within it. We take a step, lean into our apprenticeship of Jesus, and begin a path of transformation—but the seductive allure of this world, the lust of the eyes, the lust of the flesh, and the pride of life—present themselves as options. They cut in on us throughout the week and draw us off course, and before we know it, we've been side-tracked by the bad news of selfish ambition and vain conceit (see Philippians 2:3). Then we arrive at our worship experience, and the pastor, again in the proclamation of the good news of the kingdom of God, calls us away from those life-stealing stories and into the life-given story of Jesus. And we are good-newsed—evangelized.

We hear the message of the kingdom and are immediately en-amored. We long for a time when the world will be made right, when the hurt are healed, the broken are mended, the streets are safe, and opportunities for flourishing are equitably distrib-uted. However, the tensions we experience, the delay of change we see, the false prophets and pundits who promise a quick fix for what ails us leave us compromised in our commitment and allegiance to Jesus. We start to travel down paths of alliance to kingdoms of this world, fidelity to party affiliation, and we an-chor our hope in the wobbly platform of political charisma. We start to hear only what we want and see only what others pres-ent to us. We become angry and impatient with those who are the reason for our problems. We choose sides and buy into se-ductive dualisms that neatly divide the world into good and bad, the elect and the lost. Then we find ourselves embedded in a small group, taking Communion alongside those we've viewed as our opponents, watching a baptism and being reminded of our own baptismal identity, and hearing of the kingdom of God, and we are good-newsed—evangelized.

My Favorite Passage

I have both a favorite letter in the Bible and a favorite portion of that letter. We should always be careful with favoring a specific portion of the Bible, lest that portion become the lens through which we read a distorted meaning into the rest of the Bible. But with this particular passage, I'm convinced that this singular section might be one of the most important hermeneutical filters through which to read the rest of the Bible and guide the practice of our faith. I once told a congregation before I preached on this passage: "This is the key passage of my life—my 'life verses,' if you will. You can use it if you like, but just know that I hang everything I am on these verses."

Paul is writing to the church in Colossae—he's writing to the church! This is key. This passage is filled with the good news of the gospel. These words were intended to be read to the church. I am convinced this passage is evangelistic at its core. Yes, Paul's audience is already saved, but in embracing again this good news, they are also *being* saved. Regardless of the drift toward bad news—or toward what Paul calls "hollow and deceptive philosophy, which depends on human tradition and the elemental spiritual forces of this world rather than on Christ" (2:8)—Paul good-newses the Colossian church into the redemptive vision of God and the fullness of Jesus. For this is the good news.

It's the good news for each of us:
For he has rescued us from the dominion of darkness and brought us into the kingdom of the Son he loves, in whom we have redemption, the forgiveness of sins.
(1:13–14)

It's the good news anchored in the specificity of Jesus:
The Son is the image of the invisible God, the firstborn over all creation. For in him all things were created: things in heaven and on earth, visible and invisible, whether thrones or powers or rulers or authorities; all things have been created through him and for him. He is before all things, and in him all things hold together. And he is the head of the body, the church; he is the beginning and the firstborn from among the dead, so that in everything he might have the supremacy. For God was pleased to have all his fullness dwell in him, and through him to reconcile to himself all things, whether things on earth or things in heaven, by making peace through his blood, shed on the cross.
(vv. 15–20)

It remains good news if:
Once you were alienated from God and were enemies in your minds because of your evil behavior. But now he has reconciled you by Christ's physical body through death to present you holy in his sight, without blemish and free from accusation—if you continue in your faith, established and firm, and do not move from the hope held out in the gospel. This is the gospel that you heard and that has been proclaimed to every creature under heaven, and of which I, Paul, have become a servant.
(vv. 21–23)

It's good news for the whole of the cosmos:
When you were dead in your sins and in the uncircumcision of your flesh, God made you alive with Christ. He forgave us all our sins, having canceled the charge of our legal indebt-

edness, which stood against us and condemned us; he has taken it away, nailing it to the cross. And having disarmed the powers and authorities, he made a public spectacle of them, triumphing over them by the cross. (2:13–15)

Simple but Not Easy

To be saved or not to be saved? That is the question. For many of us, it's that simple. You are either saved or not. For some, true salvation guarantees the longevity of the gift. For others, salvation can be lost if one turns from the grace that saves. For both, the message is clear: through the transaction on the cross of Jesus Christ, our salvation was purchased. Acceptance of that gift guarantees one's eternal destination—perhaps, and sorta.

I've sought, likely with varying degrees of effectiveness, to illuminate a broader vision of salvation in a more holistic understanding of redemption. If God is up to something in this world, and if what God is up to is the redemption of all things, recognized in the announcement of the kingdom of God, and if this redemption is located in the life, ministry, death, and resurrection of Jesus—then salvation should have something to do with *all* of that. Paul seems to be suggesting the same in Colossians: that in Christ God has set the whole of the cosmos on a new trajectory toward redemption. My salvation is located within this big story, broad vision, and cosmic scope. Salvation is more than performing a transaction that purchases me a destination ticket. It's about a life that is caught up in the good of God's making, in receiving the good news, in participating as a good newser, and in receiving that good news over and over.

That means the question "How might I be saved?" is simple but not in the way we are accustomed to thinking about it. "How might I be saved?" is about allegiance to the One through whom the whole of the cosmos is being redeemed. It's about aligning ourselves with God's kingdom on earth as it is in heaven. It's about breaking away from the duplicitous stories and idolatrous commitments of this world. It's about the recognition of our ongoing vulnerability to corruption of character and perversity of pursuit. Even holiness, left unattended, can steadily slide toward moralism and self-righteousness. It's about committing, over and over again, to the way of Jesus, the lordship of Jesus, the kingdom manifest in Jesus. It's about living in step with the Spirit of God, through whom God's love for the world and concern for the cosmos is manifest. It's a way made possible through Jesus and a way made secure in our continuing in Jesus. One's salvation is manifest in one's participation as an ambassador of good news in this world.

Evangelism in the church is about being good-newsed often and always into this story. And it never ends! The prevalence, this side of Christ's return, of the insidious forces of corruption and perversion demands that we as the church be evangelized over and over again.

Practiced into Good Newsers through Repetitive Good News

Through our proclamation, our practices, and our performance, the church is consistently evangelized.

Each week, the church gathers for the sake of corporate worship. In this space, something should happen. It's not about an entertaining experience or a feel-good moment. It's about sharing space where we are again evangelized. It doesn't mean the pastor preaches the same message each week. It means the preacher gathers the people again to proclaim good news. The preacher speaks of the kingdom of God. She calls people into a vision of redemption. She points out the allure of the counter-stories of this world, pokes around in the uncomfortable places. She disrupts the routines of or complicity in the perversity of the world. She invites us in. She reminds us that our place is in the good news of the kingdom. We are confronted. We are convicted. We are forced to confess. We, by the grace of God, reaffirm our commitment. We consecrate our ways. And we are commissioned to be sent out into the world. We are being evangelized yet again.

Each week, the church gathers around a table, a baptistery, and a calendar that has been constructed to mark time in a redemptive, story-forming way. When we partake in Eucharist, we are being evangelized. At the Lord's Table through the broken body and the emptied blood, we are reminded of the cost of redemption. It is first Christ's cost and then ours to take up for the sake of the world. At the Table we are included again in the mystery of all ages—Christ within us, Christ for us, Christ for the world. At the Table we stand with those from all walks of life, from all different experiences and perspectives, from different worldviews and cultures, political parties, and economic status, and we are one before the Lord. We are being good-newsed out of our divisions and into our union in Christ.

In baptism, we are reminded of our own stories when we watch the story of a new apprentice of Jesus unfold before our eyes. We are reminded that we have also taken that holy plunge and, in doing so, abandoned our allegiances to the idolatrous stories, the twisted identities, and the unjust ways that proliferate the world. We are being good-newsed into our identity in Christ.

Each week in the benediction, we are being blessed as we are sent. We are reminded that our entry into the world is for the sake of the world, to bear in our bodies the blessings of redemption, the hope of goodness, and the witness to reconciliation. In having peace spoken over us, we are dispatched in the good news of God's peace-making call upon his followers. Even as we depart, we are being good-newsed, evangelized again and again, compelled to say yes again and again, believing that with every assent to God's good news we come closer and closer to the kingdom on earth as it is in heaven.

Evangelism never stops. The church lives in the constant conversion to the good news of God's kingdom, manifest in Jesus, made possible throughout the life of the church through the Spirit, all to the glory of the Father. Though the seductive allure of the powers of this world attempt to draw us away, our corporate convening realigns our perspective and helps us reimagine the possibilities of a world made new. There we receive again the Spirit-empowered capacity to be the bearers of good news in this world.

Be a good newser in a world filled with bad news! Don't peddle the mayhem and division. Care deeply. Listen intently. Watch